MEDIA
SPIRITUAL
GATEWAY

BY DR. ALAN PATEMAN

By Dr. Jennifer Pateman

Available from APMI Publications, Amazon.com and Other Retail Outlets

MEDIA
SPIRITUAL
GATEWAY

DRS. ALAN & JENNIFER PATEMAN

BOOK TITLE:
Media, Spiritual Gateway

WRITTEN BY Drs. ALAN & JENNIFER PATEMAN
Paperback ISBN: 978-1-909132-54-2
Hardcover ISBN: 978-1-909132-98-6
eBook ISBN: 978-1-909132-79-5

Published By:
APMI Publications
In Partnership with Truth for the Journey Books 24
Email: publications@alanpateman.com
www.AlanPatemanMinistries.com

Acknowledgements:
Author/Design/Senior Editor/Publisher: Apostle Dr. Alan Pateman
Editing/Proofreading/Research: Dr. Jennifer Pateman
Computer Administration/Office Manager: Dr. Dorothea Struhlik
Cover Image Credit: © khunaspix, www.fotosearch.com

Unless otherwise indicated, all scriptural quotations are from the HOLY BIBLE, NEW INTERNATIONAL VERSION ®. NIV ®. Copyright © 1973, 1978, 1984 by the International Bible Society. Used by permission of Zondervan Publishing House. All rights reserved.

*Where scriptures appear with special emphasis (**in bold,** italic or <u>underlined</u>) we have edited them ourselves in order to bring focused attention within the context of this subject being taught.*

❖

Dedication

We just want to thank our friends, partners and Executive Directors - Reverend Doctor Henry O. Ogbebor, Apostle Doctor Benjamin A. Asare and Bishop Doctor Solomon Gbakara Oghenesuvwetoba, for their love and encouragements. Not forgetting our International Administrator and Executive Dean, Doctor Dorothea Struhlik. Finally to our very special children Andrew James, Naomi and Abigail.

❖

Table of Contents

❖

Foreword

Apolitically charged climate promotes mal-practice, such as deliberately disseminated misinformation, (twisted and distorted facts), the rewriting of history and the promotion of intolerance. Racial divides are stronger than ever irrespective of all the **social-justice rhetoric** pouring out of elite places such as Hollywood and the media.

The culture war is on! One side accusing the other for being tone deaf, while the other for being biased. The lines are drawn and sentiments run deep, fed by fake facts, false narratives, deep state politics and cult-like-activism that now saturates our schools and all other learning institutions like colleges and universities. We could go on, (but you'll have to read the book!)

Politically crafted *optics* help manipulate public perception; creating an appetite for falsehood, "People loved darkness instead of light because their deeds were evil" (John 3:19 NIV).

With campaign mode ever in full-throttle, everyone everywhere has become an activist, served directly into the blood stream by the media. Homes, families, churches, communities, and entire regions have become polarised like never before. Media moguls have built empires larger than countries that monitor our every move, which is Orwellian by design.

The surge of technology especially in the field of artificial intelligence has even the top tech giants nervous. Staying ahead of the curve is their primary concern but some are also growing a conscience. Both Elon Musk and Mark Cuban have issued sharp warnings about the vulnerabilities of AI with its unstoppable power to control our lives.

Democracy is practically a myth, as we're told how to vote and reverse-psychology has gone into full effect; the media's daily pounding of Trump and his policies have only caused a *rallying-effect* that makes his base more loyal than ever. Society has never been more polarised.

After a drawn-out political season, public apathy and political-rigor-mortis usually sets in, instead the war rages on - as fresh as the day it began. Populism marches forwards and international security agencies finally denounced violent anti-fascist groups like Antifa, as domestic terrorists.

With such restlessness in the atmosphere still brooding and the blood lust of the media never winding-down, the White House's daily press briefings have digressed into feeding frenzies; while the analysts pick at the bones, the rest of us develop analysis-paralysis!

Social media continues shaping our culture (not for the better) and millennials increasingly fancy socialism and communism as a solution. We have come a long way in 50 years!

Facebook and Google ever expand in power, (yet without regulation or accountability), and have elected themselves as the universal answer to fake news. Which includes targeting and silencing Judaeo-Christian ideology and replacing conservative values and voices with liberal ones.

Double standards don't seem to matter, especially when YouTube enabled the whole world to watch the beheadings of Coptic Christians on a beach, yet recently chose to censor outspoken conservatives (and Trump Supporters) "Diamond and Silk." It hardly seems credible!

Google's company motto, "Don't be Evil," only veiled its attempts to cover up its own *anti-trust* behaviour, (for which it has been heavily sued, in Europe). Still our information is being controlled by these powerful entities, yet who's controlling them?

Our technology increases, while our morals decrease, (as Sexgate recently revealed) and the ultimate power struggle continues to rage, as medical professionals confirm how

Facebook and social media in general are ruining our brains, children and marriages (but not in that order!)

In all of these things Jesus is our surpassing victory. But we must have, "a spirit of wisdom and of revelation" in these days, so that we are not intimidated by the culture.

We must always be mindful of the, "immeasurable *and* unlimited *and* surpassing greatness of His [active, spiritual] power is in us who believe," and ever mindful that Jesus is **"far above all rule and authority and power and dominion [whether angelic or human],** and [far above] every name that is named [above every title that can be conferred], not only in this age *and* world but also in the one to come" (See Ephesians 1:16-21 AMP).

Jesus is our victory. In this age and the one to come. Amen!

❖

CHAPTER 1

Spiritual Gateway

Hello and welcome to another Truth for the Journey book. This is chapter one of an exciting subject, in regards to the implications of media and the influence that it has in society today. The scriptures are clear that this particular giant needs to be conquered, reversing the negatives that program us.

Let's start by examining Deuteronomy 7:1-2

*When the Lord brings you into the Promised Land, as he soon will, he will destroy the following seven nations, all greater and mightier than you are: **the Hittites**, the Girgashites, the Amorites, the Canaanites, the Perizzites, the Hivites, the Jebusites. When the Lord your God delivers them over to you to be destroyed, do a complete job of it —*

don't make any treaties or show them mercy; utterly
wipe them out.

(Deuteronomy 7:1-2 TLB)

Right now we are putting the spotlight on the Hittites, which is the first of seven nations mentioned above that represent seven major areas of influence that we must conquer. "He that overcometh shall inherit all things" (Revelation 21:7 KJV).

Though scripture calls them *nations,* we're going to refer to them as *spiritual gateways* and break down exactly what this spiritual gateway called "Hittite" actually stands for, so that we know what we are up against.

Conquering the Gateway of Fear & Terror

When God, your God, brings you into the country that
you are about to enter and take over, **he will clear out the**
superpowers *that were there before you: [starting with]*
the **HITTITE... Those seven nations are all bigger**
and stronger than you are. God, your God, will turn
them over to you and you will conquer them.

(Deuteronomy 7:1-2 MSG emphasis added)

The Eternal your God will put them in your power...

(Deuteronomy 7:2 VOICE)

Hebrew Definition of Hittite

Bearing in mind that Hebrew words are compound words, we must employ the aid of some great bible tools, such as the Strong's Hebrew Concordance[1] and the Brown-

Driver-Briggs' Lexicon,[2] to give us a clear definition of "Hittite," (which originates from the name "Heth,") as seen in the bible.

Put in bite-sizes like this, the implications of this particular spiritual gateway are very clear: fear, terror and discouragement.

H2850 Hebrew: chittîy *(khit-tee')*
Hittite = "descendant of Heth." The nation descended from Heth, the 2nd son of Canaan; once inhabitants of central Anatolia (modern Turkey), later in north Lebanon

H2845 Hebrew: chêth *(khayth)*
Heth = "terror" - a son of Canaan and the progenitor of the Hittites

H2865 Hebrew: châthath *(khaw-thath')*
Heth = "terror." To *prostrate;* hence to *break down,* by violence or confusion and **fear**. To abolish, affright, make afraid, amaze, beat down, discourage, cause to dismay, go down, scare, terrify. To be shattered, scared and to terrify

Who better to transport fear and terror, than the media? This spiritual gateway then represents media, which acts like a conduit that feeds negatives into our lives and methodically looks to break us down. When we are continually stunned, confused and negative, that's when we are weakest. If Satan can feed us with enough negatives daily, which we in turn run with, the rest of his dirty work is done for him. In other words, once we mount the hamster wheel of pessimism, which steadily gains momentum in our lives, it's very hard getting off!

The Media's Power to make us Negative

Media certainly has the power to wear us out with negatives, if we allow it. So we must develop a robust and impenetrable filter that protects us from the regular onslaughts of the media.

Appreciate that without the media's cooperation, things like terrorism would have no echo chamber to work with. The noise of their threats, and the images of their destruction would go largely unnoticed, and yet they continue unopposed to be broadcast across the airwaves.

While *facts* must be reported, some *facts* are conveniently sidestepped and it's no secret that the media has always had double standards. Hence the need for valid competitors that will hold the mainstream media accountable and propagate an unequivocally righteous standard.

Yet, who is willing to go? Who in this generation is saying, "Lord send me"? That's no longer referring to some distant far away mission field, but to the local, national and international media.

How the Mighty have Fallen

Sure, the fight is real. It's intense. And yes they are bigger and stronger, just like Goliath was, yet still was no match for pure hearted David. In the same way, we are told above, "God will put them in your power," "conquer them... make no treaty with them." So, who will stand up and be counted?

Who will allow God to position them, to conquer? Who is willing to slay today's Goliath - the media?

In this moment let's consider millennials, specifically those who are on fire for God, and who possess unique capabilities when it comes to technology. We are told that they are tech-savvy, digitally native and organic! But this has been *gifted* to them, by virtue of the times that they live in and the generation they were born into. Still, gifts are not to be held. Joseph could interpret dreams. That gift made way for him, but it was for the greater good, to serve the bigger picture.

On the issue of ego and narcissism, put the spotlight back on Joseph. He couldn't have gone any higher up the ladder, save becoming Pharaoh himself! But that was never the intention. So who will stick with God's blueprint, regardless? Who will die to self, long enough, to carry the mission through? Can millennials really carry this sort of responsibility? *Will...* they?

Giants do fall. And when they finally do, "Oh how the mighty have fallen!" Recently Hollywood mogul Harvey Weinstein has been toppled from his power post, for allegations of quid-pro-quo, harassment and sexually lewd misconduct stemming three decades. But in his prime, no one was willing to take him on. He was too powerful. Now, shamefaced Hollywood A-lister's are being questioned about their silent compliance and for looking the other way. Exposing just how disingenuous feminism is in Hollywood being anti-Trump but *NOT* pro-women - as they claim. Their lecturing hypocrisy glares for all to see.

The only fear that the people of God should relent to is the fear of God, although the daily tsunami of bad news steadily eats away at our defences. It takes an unbending commitment to God's truth, to keep our eyes fixed on Him.

> **Thou wilt keep him in perfect peace, whose mind is stayed on thee: because he trusteth in thee.** *Trust ye in the Lord for ever: for in the Lord Jehovah is everlasting strength:* **For he bringeth down them that dwell on high;** *the lofty city, he layeth it low; he layeth it low, even to the ground; he bringeth it even to the dust...*

> *With my soul have I desired thee in the night; yea, with my spirit within me will I seek thee early: for* **when thy judgments are in the earth, the inhabitants of the world will learn righteousness...**

> **Lord, thou wilt ordain peace for us:** *for thou also hast wrought all our works in us.*
>
> *(Isaiah 26:3-5,9,12 KJVS)*

❖

CHAPTER 2

The Definition of Media

A s we saw in chapter one, the Hebrew definition of *Hittite* was all about FEAR. Mentioned first out of seven, for good reason, as no other spiritual gateway holds as much power as the media. Fear has great sway to influence everything that goes on in society; locally, nationally and internationally, including stock markets and the global economy.

However according to Revelations 21:7-8, we are destined to conquer and not be defeated or beaten down by fear. In fact if we surrender our lives to the propaganda of fear, then God is not pleased at all.

So how do we define the media? The dictionary says that it's: "the main means of mass communication (broadcasting, publishing, and the Internet) regarded collectively." The platforms it uses are radio and TV stations, news networks and outlets, newspapers and magazines, Internet websites, opinion sites, blogs and much more.

News travels faster than the speed of light in today's world. It can circle the globe countless times before we can count on one hand! The Internet makes news not only travel faster but also greatly more accessible and widens the audience to even younger demographics, unparalleled to any other time in history.

Censorship, Monopoly and Groupthink

Part of media's power is its ability to censor information in order to control the narrative. Companies such as Facebook and Google for example, hold dangerous monopolies; even have as much revenue as some countries do! In fact Investopedia is quoted as saying, "Google's revenue beats the GDP of several major countries." Calling the company, "Google Nation" and its employees, "corporate citizens."[1]

Media can incite public outrage over political issues while at the same time muffling stories that warrant massive exposure. Interviews can be deliberately *spliced* to misrepresent and mislead.

Fake outrage can be incited. Like the crowd that demanded the release of Barabbas opposed to Jesus, (perhaps the very same crowd who shouted *"Hosanna,"* not so long before!) Media counts on the feckless and spineless principles of any *crowd.* Today, this can be referred to as *groupthink,* which according to the dictionary is, ***"the practice of*** *thinking or making decisions as a group, resulting typically in unchallenged, poor-quality decision-making."*[2]

Misinformation can be deliberately fed to the public so that by the time it's been officially *retracted* or *corrected*, the damage has long been done. Stories can be spiked or widely disseminated, depending on who is pulling the strings at the top. Partisan agendas, special interests, lobbying, bribery, elite conspiracy, cover-up and corruption, are all part of media's territory.

So it's safe to say that media, as a news outlet, is not a reliable source of impartial facts any longer, but a mechanism for *indoctrination*. Media has always flirted with danger because of its ability to shape public opinion. However, in today's environment and aggressive censorship practices, freedom of speech is either - public enemy No.1 or an elaborate myth.

Needless to say that media's reporting is not always accurate and though the use of *propaganda* is not new, it still has a new handle - *Fake-News!* Nothing exposes fake-news like politics, where elections are won and lost, based on the information that is fed to the public. The same public who take their generously cultivated *opinions* to the ballot box! Propaganda has been rebranded for today's savvier audience.

Left Leaning Media Pushes Socialism on Millennials

Conservative news and information services have been elevated in recent times, but they come under heavy fire from the left. Now more than ever, in this politically charged climate, *misrepresentation* is endemic. Take for instance socialism, which is trending specifically amongst millennials, because they have no way of grasping the consequences of going down that particular path. They have no go-to experience, in their own lifetime, to get up close to.

Learning-by-experience is lost on them because they are experiencing much of this stuff for the first time around and aren't willing to listen to the menacing warnings of history. Naïvely supposing that their new and enlightened version of socialism can offer modern improvements on a failed system that has arguably *never* worked, anywhere in the world that it has been implemented, to date. (Just ask any struggling Venezuelan who can't afford toilet paper, if they agree!)

In fact, we are going to see more of a push towards socialism as time progresses, especially from the far-left. And the more "left" of the political spectrum that the media leans, the more favourable they are going to become. After all, socialism is a control mechanism. It makes it easier to control people. While history teaches not everyone acquiesces, especially when they *realise* they're being exploited. The mainstream media that used to stand up against such things are more and more in the bag.

Tall and short of it is this: media is a major information gateway and in the wrong hands can create a dangerous monopoly. We have to offer an alternative.

We have a choice to make. Either we point out every thing that's wrong with media or we turn the tables and control this unopposed force, for good. To build up media empires that use these vastly influential means to herald the truth of God.

Joseph – God's Catalyst who went Viral!

First let's consider what aided Joseph, to live in the times that he did and not be swayed by the culture. He was a man of God who became second only to Pharaoh. His position was a result of divine strategy, even though he lived in a deeply pagan society (polytheistic and ritualistic not Judaeo-Christian). In other words his boss and counterparts didn't share his belief system!

So Pharaoh said to Joseph, "I hereby put you in charge of the whole land of Egypt." Then Pharaoh took his signet ring from his finger and put it on Joseph's finger. He dressed him in robes of fine linen and put a gold chain around his neck. He had him ride in a chariot as his second-in-command, and people shouted before him, "Make way!" Thus he put him in charge of the whole land of Egypt.

Then Pharaoh said to Joseph, "I am Pharaoh, but without your word no one will lift hand or foot in all Egypt." Pharaoh gave Joseph the name Zaphenath-Paneah and gave him Asenath daughter of Potiphera, priest of On, to be his wife. And Joseph went throughout the land of Egypt.

(Genesis 41:41-45 NIV)

What's your point? Joseph had to function deep inside an ancient Egyptian system, without it getting deep inside of him. He remained righteous and divinely positioned in order to help serve and save that society. (Not to mention, preserve the lineage of Jesus Christ).

So, Joseph was God's change-agent at a crucial juncture in history. He was the lynchpin and catalyst for systemic change, without being changed himself. This is our model. We are to go into the market place, where corruption dwells and allow God to raise us up. We need to understand God's positioning and bring His righteous influence from deep within and from the top down. Some of us are like modern Trojan horses, uniquely anointed and positioned to infiltrate the world's system from the inside out. (Not window-shopping outside-looking-in). We've got to get *inside* the culture in order to impact it - not vice-versa.

Bear in mind though, that Joseph's preparation for this position was intense. Why? He had to be able to handle it. His foundations had to run deep, so not to be toppled by the very culture he was injected into. Our God is a master strategist. He gets results, if we follow and obey His plan and not our own egos.

Pharaoh may not have changed much. Egyptian society might not have changed much, but God got His desired result. So not everyone out there in society is going to be saved, just because we show up, still God's strategy will play out, all the same.

Today God has no less ability to position his change-agents, who can go "viral" into the blood stream of society, culture and the media.

❖

CHAPTER 3

God's Plan and Purpose!

In Deuteronomy the **Hittites** were the first of a list of seven very strong nations that needed be conquered in the Promised Land. And what propagates fear, terror and dismay more than the media? (Entertainment is fiction but News is based on facts).

> *Seven nations, all greater and mightier than you are: the Hittites, the Girgashites, the Amorites, the Canaanites, the Perizzites, the Hivites, the Jebusites. When the Lord your God delivers them over to you to be destroyed, do a complete job of it.*
>
> *(Deuteronomy 7:1-2 TLB)*

In the last segment, we considered Joseph and the position he was given in Egyptian society, next to Pharaoh because of the gift that God had given him, of interpreting dreams. Beyond dreams Joseph had much more to offer and bring to the table. He was a great leader who knew how to mange things well. He was an organiser, fixer and problem solver. He handled responsibility well and got results, which benefited everyone. So interpreting dreams was just the tip of the iceberg.

The idea of going into the secular arena to bring change is synonymous with the example Joseph set. God so loved the world that He gave. We could say that He gave Joseph to Pharaoh and to the Egyptian people, to help avert a major humanitarian catastrophe. There was much more to it of course, but for our purposes here, we know that Joseph was positioned, not just for personal gain or legacy; he was fulfilling the very purposes of God in his generation, which made way for the next.

> *We know that all things work together for good to them that love God, to them who are the **called according to his purpose.***
>
> *(Romans 8:28 KJVS)*

> *We are confident that God is able to orchestrate everything to work toward something good and beautiful when we love Him and **accept His invitation to live according to His plan.***
>
> *(Romans 8:28 VOICE)*

God has a plan. But a plan always requires strategy. We are not groping in the dark or beating the air. There is a significant plan and when we come to God, we are yielding our lives to that purpose. It's a life of personal sacrifice. It's only as we lay it all down, that God can use us. "Offer your bodies as a *living sacrifice,* holy and pleasing to God, this is your true and proper worship" (Romans 12:1 NIV).

Above all my concern is that people live according to God's plan and not their own. This is authentic service. Everything outside of that is nothing more than self-service and false-humility.

True Humility Counters Narcissism

Joseph was elevated from a pit of consecration. **It takes great humility to stay dedicated in elevated positions.** Think of Daniel. He too knew how to function in a secular environment but stay inwardly holy. He was not a man of compromise, (what you compromise to keep, you'll always lose anyway!)

> *Humble yourselves, therefore, under God's mighty hand, that he may lift you up in due time.*
> *(1 Peter 5:6-7 NIV)*

> *He gives His grace [His undeserved favour] to the **humble** [those who give up self-importance].*
> *(Proverbs 3:34 AMP)*

> *It's common knowledge that "God goes against the wilful proud; **God gives grace to the willing humble."***
> *(James 4:6 MSG)*

> *All of you, clothe yourselves with humility toward one another, because, "God opposes the proud but **shows favour to the humble."***
> *(1 Peter 5:5 NIV)*

So how do we influence the media? The answer: there must be an army of Josephs and Daniels to flood the market! Men and women of personal sacrifice, who'll sacrifice personal gain for a higher purpose, in the face of cultural narcissism.

Cultural Penetration

*He said unto them, **Go ye into all the world,** and preach the gospel to every creature.*

(Mark 16:15 KJV)

*Men shall be lovers of their own selves… lovers of pleasures more than lovers of God; having a form of godliness, but denying the power thereof: **from such turn away.***

(2 Timothy 3:4 KJV)

Herein is our dilemma. How do we simultaneously, **"go INTO all the world"** and **"…turn away"** at the same time? How do we breach the culture without being snared by it? It presents us with a legitimate paradox. The only answer can be that we must *penetrate* the heart of the culture without it penetrating ours. Making no treaties and remaining solely surrendered to God.

In Mark 16:15 the original language for, *"go **into** all the world,"* directly refers to *"penetration."* The Israelites may have left Egypt but Egypt had certainly not left them. So their hearts readily gravitated back to what influenced them the most, *(and who knew cucumbers and onions tasted so good?!)*

We remember the fish we ate in Egypt at no cost — also the cucumbers, melons, leeks, onions and garlic. But now we have lost our appetite; we never see anything but this manna!

(Numbers 11: 5-6 NIV)

Thinking of the country they had left, they would have had opportunity to return.

(Hebrews 11:14-16 NIV)

In short, nothing can bring lasting change without penetration: "The *entrance* of thy words giveth light; it giveth understanding…" (Psalm 119:130 KJV) We must penetrate the culture, using media, allowing God to affect the culture forever with His incorruptible seed, because it never returns to Him void.

❖

CHAPTER 4

Cultivate Divine Connections

Who amongst us is called to the arena of media? Who is genuinely anointed and appointed and where should they begin? The answer is by getting savvy, educated and divinely placed. Networking is what the Holy Spirit specialises in. He cultivates divine connections. He knows just *how* to get you started and *where* you should begin.

In fact He's stirring a sense of urgency amongst us now, so that we recognise these people and seek to support them. There is an anointing that wants to rest on them, in this generation. Let's understand who they are, see them trained up and unleashed on the culture. Without **making them** *churchy* or ineffective.

Yes, traditionally people have tried to make all *gifts* churchy, instead of understanding their nature and their purpose. For instance the word **secular** by definition means: *the profane, worldly, irreligious, materialistic and non-spiritual.* Consequently, targeting the secular arena with a churchy strategy is futile.

"Oh well, that takes a certain type of person to go into that kind of field," I hear someone caution. Of course! It's paramount that they are CALLED first and foremost. Only such individuals have the necessary hardwiring that enables them to stand. *(We must never underestimate God!)*

And while some gifts are central to the church, the overall commission remains: **"Go into all the world,"** *not,* "go into all the church!"

Supported not Patronised

Popular radio host and best-selling author in the United States, Laura Ingraham, a long time Fox News Channel contributor, is on the cuff of hosting her own FNC show, *The Ingraham Angle* (Oct 2017).[1] In a recent interview with Pat Robertson from the 700 Club, she asked Pat for prayer, which he did directly, on air! He prayed for the anointing and the courage for her to go into that difficult arena with opposition on every side.[2]

There must be recognition like this, of the spiritual battle that rages. These people become targets indeed, but they are anointed, they can handle it. They are divinely positioned. They take on a mantle and run! We can admire their courage and spine.

Though there needs to be a greater recognition of who these people are today, so we can lay hands on them and send them out, in the right way.

In reality, individuals must get before God and recognise the gifts and calling on their own lives *(actively seeking to fulfil it)*, long before any outward recognition comes from others. Especially at first, but once there's fruit it will speak for itself,

> **By their fruit you will recognize them...** *every healthy tree bears good fruit... A good tree cannot bear bad fruit... Therefore, by their fruit you will recognize them.*
> *(Matthew 7:16-20 AMP)*

Our Consent is the Prerequisite

They must be like Joseph and Daniel, who had certain things in common. Firstly they were both educated and very dedicated individuals. Plus they both underwent intense preparation and experienced deep humiliation. Yet this did not deter them. These men were willing and obedient and God raised them both up to arenas of great responsibility.

> *If you are **willing** and **obedient,** you shall eat the best of the land.*
> *(Isaiah 1:19 AMP)*

The Hebrew word for *willingness* is: **consent** and for *obedience* is: **to hear.** This is central, because every account of victory in the bible came down to divine strategy.

It's our job to partner with God so that His will, can be accomplished on this earth as it is in heaven. But He wants our partnership to be consensual, not forced. **Obedience is *offered* not taken.** Cain and Abel showcased this fact that God won't accept obedience deprived of willingness. Notice also that *consent* comes before *hearing*. Our willingness unlocks the process. **God speaks *once* we consent** and people wonder why they never hear His voice!

Also notice that to hear is to obey. They are considered synonymous. That's because once someone hears God, they become instantly responsible!

Mostly, we like things the other way around. We want to listen *first,* and then weigh things up, whereas true faith is *available,* regardless. Like children, who only know how to follow, until they learn to distrust.

> He called a little child and set him before them, and said, "I assure you and most solemnly say to you, unless you repent [that is, change your inner self — your old way of thinking, live changed lives] and **become like children [trusting, humble, and forgiving],** you will never enter the kingdom of heaven. Therefore, **whoever humbles himself like this child is greatest in the kingdom of heaven."**
>
> (Matthew 18:2-4 AMP)

In a nutshell, it takes humility to listen, *(without wanting to speak)* and it takes humility to follow, *(without wanting to lead).* Once we give our lives to God, to serve His purposes, we have to learn to follow all over again. And before God can reveal His strategy, our willingness is the prerequisite.

Gethsemane was so central to God's plan because Jesus couldn't go to the cross without giving His personal consent. That was the condition:

The reason my Father loves me is that I lay down my life — *only to take it up again.* **No one takes it from me, but I** **lay it down of my own accord.** *I have authority to lay* *it down and authority to take it up again. This command* *I received from my Father.*

(*John 10:17-18 NIV*)

Bold Mobilization can Recapture

However willingness without strategy is dead! Moses had to climb the mountain to get the patterns from heaven to build the temple. Likewise we can only build according to God's blueprint.

Penetrating the media and the culture requires divine strategy and revelation knowledge. With an army of individuals, willing to serve God's plan, to saturate the airwaves with His thoughts, will turn the deluge of misinformation that's flooded the earth.

Except there must be *many* of us, who don't fear the media and are willing to be used by God to turn the culture back to Him. Just imagine what a difference it will make, if talented and righteous journalists start reporting unadulterated facts!

As of now, demonic powers have been reigning without resistance, and enjoying a controlling monopoly on the world's media as a governing principality that spews delusion. This generation, like no other *must* provide the tangible opposition that's been lacking. With a deep sense of priority and urgency, they must mobilise to *take* this spiritual gateway back.

> *From the days of John the Baptist until now* **the kingdom of heaven suffers violence, and the violent take it by force.**
>
> *(Matthew 11:12 KJV)*

Godly men and women make better reporters, who do a better job. With the spirit of wisdom and revelation, they can channel truth back into the blood stream of society, which will cancel out the misrepresentations, fabrications and caricatures.

Such reporting can show the whole world what true journalism looks like again, by reporting facts that haven't been twisted by demonic powers.

Remember that journalists *(including teachers)* must share facts not opinion; and educate not indoctrinate – otherwise there's no limit to their influence. Nevertheless we are not up against mere flesh and blood. The battle we face is against unseen spiritual forces that use unwitting and often conscientious people:

> *Our struggle is not against flesh and blood [contending only with physical opponents], but against the rulers, against the powers, against the world forces of this [present] darkness, against the spiritual forces of wickedness in the heavenly (supernatural) places.*
>
> *(Ephesians 6:12 AMP)*

❖

CHAPTER 5

As Goes America
So Goes the World

As the most advanced democracy on the globe America's influence on the rest of the world is real. In other words, what happens in America eventually filters down on the rest of us, for better or for worse. In that light, we want to capture what's happening in the news media right now, because the impact and repercussions run deep.

And we can't write about the global news media service without mentioning current events, starting with America. At the time of writing, this includes the media's intense and visceral hatred of President Donald Trump, 93% negativity rate. Certainly not fair and not balanced.

Political Tribalism fed by Media Bias

An article, **"How much does CNN hate Trump? 93% of Coverage is Negative,"** written by Joseph Curl, of The Washington Times, May 2017, discusses the disproportionately negative coverage:

"For the youngsters out there, once upon a time, CNN was pretty much down the middle. The fledgling network covered news — real news, not fake news — and worked hard to be on site wherever news was happening. When something happened, that was the place to go.

But those days are long gone. Watch any 10 minutes of CNN, and now you'll see nothing more than a nonstop — and often vicious — diatribe against President Trump.

Under the lead of former NBC head Jeff Zucker, **CNN has become a far-left network that harangues the right and praises the left, almost nonstop. 'News' is secondary. Now it's all about pushing an agenda and toeing the line for the liberal overlords.**

Case in point: Harvard released a study last week that analysed The New York Times, The Wall Street Journal, The Washington Post and the main newscasts on CBS, CNN, Fox and NBC during Mr Trump's first 100 days. No shocker here: 80 percent was negative, just 20 percent positive.

That's a big change from the past. When the Chosen One, Barack Obama, completed his first 100 days, a similar study found that coverage was 59 percent positive, 41 percent negative. Skewed, but not that bad. The numbers were flipped for George W. Bush, of course: 57 percent negative, 43 percent positive. For Bill Clinton, way back in 1993, in the days when news was news (which means reporters were hard on the President regardless of his political affiliation), the coverage was 60 percent negative, 40 percent positive.

'The Harvard team found that CBS coverage was 91 percent negative and 9 percent positive. New York Times coverage was 87 percent negative and 13 percent positive,' Byron York wrote in the Washington Examiner. 'Washington Post coverage was 83 percent negative and 17 percent positive. Wall Street Journal coverage was 70 percent negative and 30 percent positive. And Fox News coverage also leaned to the negative, but only slightly: 52 percent negative to 48 percent positive.'"[1]

I like what Laura Ingram calls it, "the-perpetual-grievance-factory." Fake moral-outrage is par-for-the-course these days and it's the media that predominantly feeds it. Not to mention all the other "fake" issues out there, such as fake-feminism, (I'll leave that subject for my wife to address in her next book!)

Journalists - Gatekeepers
For the Political Ruling Class

John Kass, of the Chicago Tribune also wrote: "Whenever I mention the news media leans ridiculously far to the left, that it has lost half the country with its attitude and that the tone of the coverage of President Donald Trump is over-the-top hostile, I get the same darn reaction. The eye-roll. That big Anderson Cooper CNN eye-roll, often accompanied by a few theatrical sighs. And when I leave the newsroom, it gets even worse on social media…"

He continues, **"CNN and NBC struck a 93 percent negative tone on their Trump stories, with only 7 percent positive.** CBS was third in the anti-Trump race, with a 91 to 9 ratio. And the pro-Trump Fox News? That network was 52 percent negative to 48 percent positive. So what does fair and balanced really mean, anyway?

The response will be that Trump is deserving of this kind of coverage because he's conducted himself inappropriately, and these are self-inflicted wounds, and the press is doing nothing but covering him and his actions. But that's a little bit disingenuous… And now the establishment kicks back.

Many beltway journalists are essentially establishment creatures, *gatekeepers* for the political ruling class, members of that class and fierce guardians of their place in the empire. The political class sees Trump and the 62 million Americans who voted for him as the stuff they scrape off their shoes…

I have my own memory of the media's tone after Obama took office. It wasn't merely positive, **it was adoring, gushy, in the way a small child looks up to a beloved parent, or a dog to the master who gives it biscuits.**

It was as if the media were hugging a magical unicorn. Obama wasn't only given the benefit of the doubt. **He was handed the Nobel Peace Prize though he hadn't done anything to earn it. And critics were trashed as nothing but racists.**

Obama controversies, from his administration's gun running scandal in the 'Fast and Furious' debacle to using the Internal Revenue Service as a weapon against conservative groups, were covered, somewhat. **But generally, the tone was muted, respectful; nothing like it was for Trump or the Clintons.**

Later, in Hillary Clinton's failed 2016 campaign, leaks of Democratic National Committee email — whether hacked by the Russians or not — demonstrated collusion between journalists and Democrats. But that cozy relationship has never properly been addressed, and **that avoidance undermines the credibility of journalism** as the media challenges Trump.

'Because of the way the press covered Obama, they lost so much credibility,' Bevan said. 'And because they did not take these things seriously, the IRS Scandal, Fast and Furious, you could go down the list of where they turned the other cheek... And now where they're giving Trump the third degree on everything that makes the contrast all that much greater.

So you have a certain segment of the public, the people who voted for Trump, who literally do not trust what the media says.' And the divide between rigidly defined **political tribes,** one courted by the media, the other dismissed by it, grows even wider. **'It's not good for journalism, and it's not good for the country,'** said Bevan."[2]

The Scandal Rich

Dominating the newsreel, other than Trump, is the Clintons machine. Always flirting with controversy. The

Clinton playbook is, *"Catch me if you can!"* Blame game tactics and smoke screens politics are standard practice.

Originally, journalism was intended to hold authority figures accountable, especially those in the government (adversarial press). But with a long history of controversies and scandals where they have looked the other way and not done their job (given free-passes for partisan agendas), it's easy to see that most journalists are actually political activists today and many have been *bought-and-paid-for*.

We're choosing to use American politics to prove this point about the media bias, simply because the 2016 campaign, revealed to the rest of the world - in spectacular fashion - just how blatantly corrupt American politics has become (which filters down on the rest of us). Still, no one is naïve enough to suggest that Europe is any better.

To continue, not all journalists enjoy having their profession so deeply undermined. Kyle Smith for example, of the National Review wrote of Hillary's long list of lies, which just keeps giving, saying:

> "She has no idea why many Americans think 'Clintonian' is another way of saying 'dishonest'... **Lying is an involuntary reflex for the Clintons, like sneezing...** She blithely lists good deeds done by the Clinton Foundation without defending or even mentioning the controversial cases in which she apparently did favours for donors in deals that **caused Andrew C. McCarthy to liken her State Department to 'a racketeering enterprise.'**

For Hillary, it's the equivalent of O. J. Simpson's protesting that there were lots of days on which he didn't murder his ex-wife."[3]

This is a short list of *some* of the many *indiscretions* of the Clinton/Obama era that come to my mind:

- Monica Lewinsky scandal - led to 2nd ever impeachment of US President
- The Clinton Foundation favours: a pay-to-play back door to the State Department - an open checkbook for foreigners to curry favour
- Bill's Golden Tongue: His/her speech fees that shocked the public
- The Clinton's Private Email Server
- Clinton's State Department Emails
- Benghazi
- Fast and Furious
- Uranium One
- Iran deal ($ billions)
- Weaponising the IRS - against conservative groups such as the Tea party
- Wire tapping and unmasking
- Mr Clinton's and former Attorney General, Loretta Lynch's "tarmac meeting"
- Dirty and *expensive* Opposition Research

- Bogus Dossier – paid for by the DNC and the Clinton campaign (Christopher Steele Ex-MI6/Fusion GPS etc.)
- Led to Muller's Special Counsel Russia Investigation
- Massive Conflicts of interest
- And on and on and on!

It's difficult to believe that this list is hardly exhaustive. And that if the media had done their job, more would have come to light sooner. The old adage goes: **"The best disinfectant is sunlight."** Better still, "There is nothing hidden that will not become evident, nor *anything* secret that will not be known and come out into the open" (Luke 8:17 AMP).

As for the Uranium One or the Iran deal, it's hard to understand the motivation behind these events, (collusion perhaps!) It can only be one of two things: country or money. As Andrew McCarthy said, "The Russian company sought to acquire a controlling interest in Uranium One. That would mean a takeover not only of the Kazakh mines but of the U.S. uranium assets as well. **Secretary Clinton approved the Russian takeover."**[4]

❖

CHAPTER 6

Collusion and the Jezebel Spirit

Is collusion even a crime? The short answer is, NO! But if one wants to find collusion, one needs to look no further than the Clintons. Peter Schweizer in his blockbuster exposé and New York Times Bestseller called, **"Clinton Cash: The Untold Story of How and Why Foreign Governments and Businesses Helped Make Bill and Hillary Rich,"** uncovered some troubling facts behind the Clinton money trail, the official corruption in Washington and "the Clinton's troubling dealings in Kazakhstan, Colombia, Haiti, and other places at the 'wild west' fringe of the global economy… and possible indebtedness to an array of foreign interests."

The mainstream media have been complicit, in that they have showed substantial bias and enjoyed way too much power. It's time to turn things around.

The revelations of government level racketeering and criminal cartel activity that exceeds Watergate, has less power to shock and excite and **something far more sinister is happening; we are becoming indifferent.**

The world's media have all danced to the beat of the same drum and been complicit with all the corruption, in an attempt to cover up, mute and dangerously censor political opponents. The most used word in 2017 has been the word FAKE, because fake media is based on fear, deception and a Jezebel spirit (rebellion, witchcraft, control, seduction and mass-manipulation).

Bring True Journalism Back

We've all seen journalism done badly. We know what that looks like. Nevertheless, in their defence, journalists who do their job properly are *friend* not *foe*. Especially if they're truly dedicated to broadcasting truth and not lies, for a living. Remember facts that have been twisted and distorted are now lies. **Anything *misrepresented* is like poison; it only takes one drop to poison the whole well.**

Good investigative journalism is to be applauded not feared. Journalism done well has managed to expose some of the deepest corruptions in history. Journalists worth their salt are some of the most hard working and genuine people, who have put their lives in danger in order to expose scandals and exploitation that the world needs to know about. And we need these people. In fact God will use them, for His own purposes.

So from Watergate to Russiagate or allegations of racketeering at the highest level, (fraud, money laundering, kick-backs, pay-for-play and so on); journalists are the ones to expose it. And again I say we need journalists, who will operate out of righteous indignation and not cave to the corruption.

Adversarial Journalism

We couldn't write a book about the media without putting the spotlight on adversarial journalism, as it is so prevalent today, like never before. And looking for a good definition to help explain this particular genre of journalism, we found the following written by Matthew Helmer, who describes it as, "One of the most popular journalism forms we see in media today."

He goes on to say, "Screaming, finger pointing, and accusations... In today's media, we have come to expect a level of bravado in our journalism. But when did all this start? **Adversarial journalism** is the official term for investigative reporting done in an antagonistic way. Although some forms of adversarial journalism can be overly biased and even abusive, adversarial journalism has also helped to expose a number of important scandals...

History of Adversarial Journalism:

Adversarial journalism has been around since before the birth of the United States. During the Revolutionary War, proponents for American independence published articles that exposed embarrassing or damaging details about British colonial leaders. During the late 19th and early 20th centuries, the term **yellow journalism** was used to describe sensational headlines that lacked journalistic integrity. In 1906, President Theodore Roosevelt famously used the disgusting-sounding term **muckraking,** to describe reporters' efforts to find 'dirt' on politicians, policies, and political machines.

Roosevelt saw muckrakers as unpleasant but necessary journalists in a democratic society. Early work by muckrakers included breaking up oil monopolies, passing food and drug regulations, and child labor laws based on their ability to investigate controversial issues.

Adversarial Journalism and Today's News Reporting:

Adversarial journalism today is ruled by cable news. To fill the need for 24 hours of constant content, news channels have turned to adversarial journalism in order to boost ratings. Top rated shows... feature confrontational hosts with strong opinions on political issues, who go to battle with their adversaries. These types of journalists are known as pundits, and they have blended fact, opinion, and especially entertainment in news reporting.

Interview techniques by adversarial journalists include searching for controversial sound bites, manipulation of quotes and statistics, adopting an argumentative and combative dialogue, and attempting to catch your opponent in a misstep.

Adversarial journalism is perfect for television because it is able to present itself as news while at the same time

providing entertainment. **Critics of adversarial journalism have stated it has resulted in increased partisanship, a lack of objectivity, and that it has killed investigative journalism."**[1]

Antifa - Useful Idiots for the Political Elite

Admittedly uncorroborated conspiracy theories are never helpful, regardless of which side of the political aisle you're on. Especially when such theories get *breathlessly* fed into the public blood stream, unchecked, which recklessly breeds division and violence.

Not helped by fake-news outlets claiming that, "The Whitehouse has been occupied by White Supremacists!" Thus giving rise to one particular ugly consequence called Antifa. (A fast growing anti-fascist group that's officially recognised as a *domestic terrorist organisation in the US*).

Antifa is not unique to the States of course. We are currently living in Tuscany, Italy and we woke up one morning to find that all our neighbouring buildings had new bright red graffiti on them, in big letters that spelt "ANTIFA." This was right on our doorstep, logistically and we're in the very heart of Europe here.

Browsing recently on Craigslist we saw this random statement, which read quote:

"Alt-Left Icon Vladimir Lenin called them 'Useful Idiots,' Generals call them 'Cannon Fodder.' In Seattle they're hiring 'Resist Activists' with preferences for the mentally ill...!"

Not so funny, perhaps, yet it highlights a valid point. If you're not familiar with the term "useful idiot" it originated with Vladimir Lenin, whose attitude towards communist sympathisers in the West, was not so kind! While Lenin and the Soviets held them in utter contempt they also viewed them as *instruments* for distributing their communist propaganda to other countries, infecting other cultures with their totalitarian rhetoric. After the mission was achieved, such *"idiots"* were no longer *"useful."*

Likewise, today's left-leaning political elites, (such as George Soros and others), allegedly secretly fund but don't openly support Antifa. And why would they condemn the violence, when it's *useful* to their political scheming.

Back in August 2017, after protests at Berkeley, Steve Forbes posted on his Twitter, **"Stop Making Excuses for Antifa Thuggery,"** with an attached article from the National Review, which read in part: "There will always be thugs who enjoy breaking things and hurting people. **The real scandal is that otherwise respectable people are willing to look the other way or explain away the violence, so long as its perpetrators are on their side.** They are just as cowardly as the mask-wearing antifa thugs who are brave enough to punch and kick people, but not to show their faces."[2]

Definition of Antifa:

The online Urban Dictionary rarely holds anything back! Yet I was surprised to find that on this open forum, not many were sympathetic towards this particular group, at all. Here are just some of the top definitions that were given, at the time of writing (and don't forget to read the hashtags):

Skankhunt81 defined Antifa as: "The purest form of contradiction, hypocrisy, and accidental irony; they are the modern day equivalent of Nazis. 'Hey I'm antifa, I'll pepper spray you for not conforming to my socialist/communist/anarchist ideology.'"
#antifa #imspecialcuzihatetrump #losers #irony #contradiction #hypocrisy #idiots #sheep
(Posted October 12, 2017)

Ikampsowhatfu defined Antifa as: "Short for Anti Fascists: Excrement throwing wanna-be freedom fighters... Typically live with their parents. Some are communistic college professors. Spout idiotic, meaningless slogans against police, and conservatives. Answer ads in craigslist to rent a mob for 15-20 bucks an hour. Stink. 'Antifa is throwing poop like monkeys again.'"
(Posted October 12, 2017)

And finally **Soldier of Eden** said they were: "A bunch of terrorist thugs that will cry and burn stuff down until they get their way, usually liberal snowflakes."[3]
#liberal #snowflake #terrorists
(Posted September 20, 2017)

Who has the Biggest Bully Pulpit?

So while the President of the United States is accused of using the biggest bully pulpit in the world, the news media are using theirs. By backing a failed campaign they felt cheated and so did Hillary, because the election didn't go their way, (even with all of the big money, lucrative back-room-deals, corruption and bribery, not to mention top celebrity collaboration). Imagine, not even Obama, (aka campaigner-in-chief), could bag the White House for Hillary. But oh how self-assured and cocky they all were!

It's evident that Hillary felt so *entitled*. It was an automatic assumption that she should *inherit* the throne, because somehow she deserved it. Especially since she helped broker so many powerful foreign deals during her tenure as Secretary of State. *Everything* was a prelude to her sole ambition.

However, she let a lot of people down. And like Jezebel, she had to save face, by discrediting and blaming EVERYONE involved. (Notice how all *useful-idiots* tend to get thrown under the political bus, once they fulfil their purpose. *Anyone* is a potential scapegoat).

Again, I repeat, "AS GOES AMERICA, SO GOES THE WORLD." All of this has had a negative impact on the rest of the world. And after lecturing the public for many months about how terrible Russia is and what a hostile foe Putin is, we are left baffled as to why the Obama administration sold 20% of America's Uranium to this same said MONSTER. This stuff would make a hypocrite blush! And once again, the media have been complicit.

So who stood to gain the most if Hillary got in? What specifically did the media stand to gain? Or who was controlling the media and the flow of information traveling through this powerful spiritual gateway?

We cannot be indifferent towards or naïve about the Clinton scandals and the media's complicity, because the results could be catastrophic. For instance, Putin would be very happy to sell America's uranium to its enemies. In fact he was trying to corner the global market for uranium by creating a monopoly.

Ultimately this Uranium One deal is clearly poised to backfire on the US. Iran and North Korea are big named players that Russia would gladly sell uranium to.

Crazy stuff! The facts are in. So it begs the question, yet again, of the Obama administration: whose side were you on? What was the real motive - the country or money? "The love of money is a root of all kinds of evil. Some people, eager for money, have wandered from the faith and pierced themselves with many griefs" (1 Timothy 6:10-NIV).

This fake-news media have fed a lethal narrative that's helping to usher in the end times, by creating events conducive with an apocalypse - Third World War or a nuclear holocaust that would by definition be ten times the scale of Hiroshima. We can't forget that dark and sinister spiritual forces are at play and using politicians and news media to do their bidding, (as useful idiots!)

> For our struggle is not against flesh and blood [contending only with physical opponents], but against the rulers, against the powers, against the world forces of this [present] darkness, against the spiritual **forces** of wickedness in the heavenly (supernatural) **places**.
> (Ephesians 6:12 AMP)

This is no afternoon athletic contest that we'll walk away from and forget about in a couple of hours. **This is for keeps, a life-or-death fight to the finish against the Devil and all his angels.**

(Ephesians 6:12 MSG)

The liberal news media downplay all conspiracy theories, except those they authorise. Yet this life-or-death battle is no game, it's for keeps. And life is no dress-rehearsal. Corrupt politicians with the aid of a corrupt news media, do irreversible damage, with irreversible consequences, including nuclear ambitions.

Bring Brexit into the mix and the power struggle that goes on in the EU, then we can understand that this spiritual struggle is a global one. And those known as the globalists understand that in order to gain absolute control, there must be an *in-gathering* or a *coming-together* of like mindedness.

One currency, one religion, one media, one authorised source of information, one government, one education, one gender, one identity, one culture, one opinion, one acceptable and politically correct tone; *one, one, one…* The New Agers call it the, "One World Order," which **claims *diversity* yet promotes cultural and global homogenization instead.**

❖

CHAPTER 7

Promoting Diversity or Global Homogenization?

In short, *homogenization* comes from the word, *homogeneous – (Greek homogenes: homos meaning* **same** + *genos meaning* **kind**) and refers to *sameness* and *uniformity.* Yes milk can be homogenised but so can society! In fact the globalists seek one big happy homogenous society, where everyone has the same rights, same access to education, the same opportunities and even the same laws. Included though, is the same *culture,* which means diversity is progressively and purposely reduced, *"limiting barriers to communication."*

We used to refer to this concept as, "global village." Which is useful for controlling trade, marketing but also individuality, innovative thinkers and new ideas. Yet this is not a new concept, considering the pre-modern or traditional forms of globalism and globalisation (that sought to colonise every inch of the globe), such as the Roman Empire in the second century and perhaps the Greeks of the fifth-century BC (just two examples).

What benign sounding word *sameness* is - so homely and comforting! Yet is it? *Same,* is only good when things are *meant* to be the same. **But anything forced into *sameness* can be cultish and even dangerous. We're going to look at why.**

Ecclesiastes 3:11 in the NIV states: **"He made everything appropriate in its time.** He also placed eternity within them — yet, no person can fully comprehend what God is doing from beginning to end." (The King James Version uses the word, "beautiful" instead). This means that true diversity, exists with God, in His kingdom. Everything else is counterfeit - a good attempt at copying the real thing.

Now consider such a mundane thing as milk. It is said of milk that when you homogenise it, you not only change the size of its fat globules, you also rearrange its fat and protein molecules, which alter how they behave inside the human body. Studies as far back as the 70s have revealed that homogenization can possibly increase the risk of heart disease.

This begs the question: **"Just because we *can* do something, does that mean we should do it?"** We might have the technology, but should milk be homogenised? Some things are supposed to be different, for all the right reasons. *Sameness* is not always appropriate, even though it might make something more aesthetically pleasing.

Relentless Media Blasting to Homogenise Society:

So how does homogenization really work? Well, the most basic explanation, without over simplifying it, is that the process includes *blasting* molecules to be of *uniform* size so they can blend together more easily without re-separating, and can remain in a state of forced-conformity. The homogeniser literally forces milk at very high pressure through very small holes. (We will explain why this is relevant).

In other words, the cream no longer separates itself from the rest of the milk, with its distinct flavour and texture. Instead it has the *same* consistency right the way through. It's no longer naturally yellow-ish in colour but a perfectly even-white colour, which has more shelf-appeal. But this takes all the fun out of it. I have memories of my brothers and I competing over the cream at the top for our breakfast cereal. It was rich, smooth and worth fighting for!

Likewise, homogenization happens in society when we are *blasted* daily by the media, who want us all to think the *same*. They do this by relentlessly banging-away at their time-honoured-profession of misinforming the people by manipulating and deliberately distorting information. It's little wonder that society is being browbeaten into submission by the press. Cutting us down to size (literally) to fit the mould and the dictates of this culture.

Heavily Filtered through Pressure and Distortion

Extreme filtering is like censorship and in a year like 2017 when "fake-news" played such a big role, fact-checking has never been more important. So I want to share an article from, Natural News, which confirms just how long conventional wisdom has taught us that, "…milk is a 'perfect food,' for building strong bodies in children and preventing osteoporosis as we age."

Yet to recalibrate our thinking, the article goes on to say: "The modern dairy products that are available in most supermarkets are nothing like the unpasteurized, un-homogenized milk of yesteryear, however. **Today's milk looks the same, but it is not the same product…**

Homogenization is a more recently invented process and it has been called 'the worst thing that dairymen did to milk.' **When milk is homogenized, it is pushed through a fine filter at pressures of 4,000 pounds per square inch. In this process, the fat globules are made smaller by a factor of ten times or more."**

Why is this a problem? Because when we tamper with God's design, the results aren't always favourable: **"Milk is a hormonal delivery system. When homogenized, milk becomes very powerful and efficient at bypassing normal digestive processes** and delivering steroid and protein hormones to the human body (both your hormones and the cow's natural hormones and the ones they may have been injected with to produce more milk).

Homogenization makes fat molecules in milk smaller and they become 'capsules' for substances that are able to bypass digestion. Proteins that would normally be digested in the stomach are not broken down and instead they are absorbed into the bloodstream."

I hear some people say, *"It's just milk, come-on!"* But for the rest of us, we have become far too discerning for that. We want to know if this factory-food is really edible or not. The trouble is, milk is no longer milk. It's more like chemical soup or a science project!

Considering the use of the word "capsule," I know my wife would suggest that our food has been "weaponised!" (God completely healed her of multiple allergies, one of which was a severe milk allergy, so this article is close-to-home).

It concludes with sober warnings: "Proteins were created to be easily broken down by digestive processes. Homogenization disrupts this and insures their survival so that they enter the bloodstream. Many times the body reacts to foreign proteins by producing histamines, and then mucus. **Sometimes homogenized milk proteins resemble a human protein and can become triggers for autoimmune diseases such as diabetes or multiple sclerosis.**

Two Connecticut cardiologists have demonstrated that homogenized milk proteins did in fact survive digestion. It was discovered that Bovine Xanthene Oxidase (BXO) survived long enough to affect **every one of three hundred heart attack victims over a five-year time period. Even**

young children in the U.S. are showing signs of hardening of the arteries."[1]

Fake Peace - Don't Offend the Culture!

So it's not just things like milk and soft drinks like cola that suffer intense homogenization; our lives experience intense pressure too. My analogy has managed to take us from fake milk - to fake society (synthetically contrived culture), but this would include fake unity too. Everyone is afraid to offend the culture and can no longer enjoy autonomous thinking, because social-media is slowly but crudely cloning us all into fake thinkers! Where we all use the same superficial talking points and all think the same.

The political polls that used to be so heavily relied upon during election cycles have lost much of their credibility, because they got it **totally wrong** during Brexit and during the American presidential campaign in 2016. Trump had, "no path to victory" and Clinton was going to win "without a doubt."

What that revealed more than anything else was that (besides the fact that polls have become irrelevant in a changing society and new methods need to be developed); people were not honest. **Trump had a lot of silent supporters.** For fear of reprisal, voters told telephone pollsters one thing and voted the opposite, in the privacy of the voting booth! The same was true during Brexit.

After both elections, Trump supporters and Brexit voters were scorned and shamed. Yet lying to the pollsters paid off because they got to keep their anonymity, (wise move!) Therefore, in this politically charged climate, polls can never be viewed in the same light again.

Scripture Exposes Fake Peace:

> *They lead my people astray, saying,* **"Peace," when there is no peace,** *and because, when a flimsy wall is built, they cover it with whitewash…*
>
> (Ezekiel 13:10 NIV)

> *The false prophets of Israel who prophesied deceitfully about Jerusalem, seeing visions of* **peace for her when there is no peace.**
>
> (Ezekiel 13:16 AMPC)

> *They dress the wound of my people as though it were not serious. "Peace, peace," they say, when there is no peace.*
>
> (Jeremiah 8:11 NIV)

> **Prophets and priests and everyone in between twist words and doctor truth.** *My dear Daughter — my people — broken, shattered, and yet they put on Band-Aids, Saying,* **"It's not so bad. You'll be just fine." But things are not "just fine!"** *Do you suppose they are embarrassed over this outrage? Not really. They have no shame. They don't even know how to blush.*
>
> (Jeremiah 8:11-12 MSG)

When the media and the cultural "tone-police" govern everything a populace expresses, feels or thinks; it's time to realise that we're being monitored for our conformity levels. The media are out to make public examples of those who don't conform to the culture, by destroying their businesses and reputation. Such as the cake baker who chose not to bake a cake for a same sex marriage ceremony, who naively thought that his *"right to choose"* was protected by law! But he was found guilty in the court of *public opinion* long before it ever reached the tangible courts.

The global media today plays a huge role in globalization. The list is long, from Sky and the BBC, to Fox, CNN, MSNBC, ABC, RT, Aljazeera, Euro News, etc., they all promote some form of propaganda and push a chosen message.

Most read from the same song sheet, (depending which way they lean politically). They're all being fed the same information; they're all using the same rhetoric. They all created a similar caricature of Trump, with few exceptions.

❖

CHAPTER 8

Democracy Debunked

Democracy is being done away with, even in the EU because elites are actually controlling *everything*. It is democracy versus the elite establishment, not just in the US but also all over the world.

In fact democracy is a myth. We are not free to make our own decisions about anything. Instead we are governed by the PC-police, the thought-police and now even the tone-police. In other words, not only are our actions being monitored and steered but even our thoughts; how to think, what to say, how to vote, etc.

The risk of non-conformity is negative *branding*. When we refuse to conform to the elite endorsed *group-think* we are branded as: irredeemables or basket-of-deplorables! Perhaps even as fascists, racists, bigots and intolerant, xenophobic, homophobic, privileged, white supremacist, misogynistic or sexist, even ageist and the list goes on.

Consequently fear drives conformity:

> *For the Spirit God gave us **does not make us timid (cowardice, fearfulness, dread, faithless) but gives us power,** love and self-discipline.*
> > *(2 Timothy 1:7 NIV Strong's added)*

> ***Do not conform (fashion one's self according to) the pattern of this world,*** *but be transformed by the renewing of your mind.*
> > *(Romans 12:2 NIV Strong's added)*

One of the worst kept secrets is the existence of such groups as the Illuminate, consisting of elite globalists, who want to usher in their One World Order (with one currency and one religion etc.)

Babel - Fake Unity and the Great Scattering

> *"Come, let us build ourselves a city, with a tower that reaches to the heavens, so that we may make a name for ourselves; **otherwise we will be <u>scattered</u> over the face of the whole earth."***

> *But the Lord came down to see the city and the tower the people were building. The Lord said, **"If as one people speaking the same language they have begun to do this, then nothing they plan to do will be impossible for them.** Come, let us go down and confuse their language so they will not understand each other."*

So the Lord <u>scattered</u> them from there over all the earth, and <u>they stopped building</u> the city. That is why it was called Babel — because there the Lord confused the language of the whole world. From there the Lord <u>scattered</u> them over the face of the whole earth.

(Genesis 11:4-9 NIV)

Notice how the word *"scattered"* is used on three consecutive occasions in just a short passage of scripture. That means there's an emphasis. Only as people come together can they achieve, (for good or for evil) and God chose to *"scatter"* them. They are still resisting this today; the globalists want everyone to be "one" in a forced unity. **They claim to want** *diversity,* **when really they demand** *conformity.*

"Straight White Men need not Apply." Such is the open hypocrisy of the DNC (the party of diversity), which recently excluded cisgender straight white males in their recruiting process:

"The Democratic National Committee is hiring for some new positions in their Technology Team, including Chief Security Officer, IT Systems Administrator, and Product Manager. In the email soliciting job applications, it says that the DNC is looking for a *'staff of diverse voices and life experiences.'*

Unfortunately, according to the DNC's Data Service Manager Madeleine Leader, this desire for *'diverse voices and life experiences'* apparently doesn't extend to *'cisgender straight white males.'* In the closing paragraph of the email, Leader said *'I personally would prefer that you not forward to cisgender straight white males, as they are already in the majority.'"*

Christine Rousselle of Townhall.com asks, "Was it really necessary to straight-up single out a group of people who shouldn't apply? If the best candidate for the job is a straight white male, they should hire the straight white male. His hypothetical, 'life experiences' aren't any less valuable due to his sexuality or skin tone and could certainly contribute to a diverse workplace. Anyhow, for what it's worth, saying this is potentially a violation of the DNC's own policies."[1]

Definition:
Cisgender is a term that refers to someone who identifies with the gender that was assigned to them at birth, i.e. someone who is *not* transgender.

Negative Caricatures only Breed Hatred

MSNBC host Joe Scarborough said of President Trump that he was a, "thug," "goon" and "embarrassment," all because of his unusual handshake with French President Emmanuel Macron of France. He went on to say that President Trump "mauled" him, which was a complete lack of respect for his office. The purpose is all about creating a negative and lasting caricature of the President.

While everyone uses branding (because it works), the left are well known for their use of **identity politics.** They constantly use the race and sex cards, which is odd when they are usually guiltier than those they point the finger at. (Just let me say two words: B.I.L.L - C.L.I.N.T.O.N!)

Yet the media go along with everything the left serves up, fanning the flames of social division, which is increasingly violent. Tensions run high when even random public events suddenly turn nasty due to politics. It's a sad reality.

CHAPTER 9

The Media & Artificial Intelligence in the End Times Part 1

Accurding to the English Oxford Dictionary the short definition for AI is: "The theory and development of computer systems able to perform tasks normally requiring human intelligence, such as visual perception, speech recognition, decision-making, and translation between languages."[1]

Unless we intend to live under a rock, the rest of us would recognise that our lives will be directly impacted by the power of the media, one way or another, from the distortion of history - to current events. This will ultimately include the coming tidal wave of artificial intelligence, that's yet to fully descend on us. And according to Elon Musk and Mark Cuban, we've seen nothing yet. But allow me to explain.

To begin with, I want to draw our attention to recent developments in China, one in particular that was called, City Brain. According to the New York Post, **"For the last year, the people of Hangzhou, China – a city of more than nine million – have had every moment of their lives tracked.** 'City Brain,' an artificial intelligence system that interlinks with a city's infrastructure was installed in October 2016, through a partnership with Alibaba and Foxconn.

In an effort to optimize Hangzhou and make urban life easier, **the system tracked everything** from robberies to traffic jams and learned the city's unique patterns and needs. Residents were also tracked through their activity on social media. Their commutes, purchases, interactions and movements were all learned and absorbed by the AI database.

Xian-Sheng Hua, (an AI manager at Alibaba), eerily predicted during a presentation at the World Summit AI meeting: **'In China, people have <u>less concern with privacy</u>, which allows us to move faster.'"**

("Move faster" for what exactly? Controlling peoples' lives!) The article continues: "According to **New Scientist,** the system works. Crime, car crashes and rush hour traffic is all down. The system can predict traffic jams and adjust the traffic lights in order to avoid congestion before it begins. It can also keep track of criminals, making it easier for police to catch them. And it automatically notifies authorities when it detects so much as an illegally parked car.

The system is also hooked up to residents' cell phones and can alert them of bad weather or traffic jams and offer safer routes. **City Brain has apparently been such a success that it's already being packaged for other cities across China and, <u>eventually, the world.</u>**"[2]

George Orwell's 1984

To quote again, **"City Brain has apparently been such a success that it's already being packaged for other cities across China and, *eventually, the world.*"** What a dark prediction! However, as extreme as this may sound, the open monitoring and surveillance of human beings within progressive societies, began a long time ago.

In fact former journalist turned author, George Orwell (Eric Arthur Blair), foresaw this eventuality and wrote about it in his novel **Nineteen Eighty Four,** which gave a snapshot of life lived under such scrutiny and is still considered one of the great dystopian satires of the 20th century.

Increasingly we hear that modern society has become more and more, "Orwellian." So let's break this down:

"Orwellian is an adjective describing a societal condition, idea or situation that George Orwell identified as being destructive to the welfare of a free and open society. It denotes an attitude and a **brutal policy of draconian control by <u>propaganda,</u> <u>surveillance,</u> <u>misinformation,</u> <u>denial of truth,</u> and <u>manipulation of the past,</u>** including the 'unperson'—a person whose past existence is expunged from the public record and memory, practised by modern repressive governments..."[3]

Propaganda, surveillance, misinformation, denial of truth, and the manipulation of history and past events - all sounds so familiar. It's right out of today's political playbook. The M.O of many governments has long been the covert (secret) surveillance of its own people, but the time is here or fast approaching, when such surveillance will be *covert* no more. (In fact open surveillance has already been normalised).

In the face of terrorism and other blights on society, the need for surveillance *conveniently increases,* while all opposition to it *conveniently decreases.* This is by design not by default. Fear causes people to capitulate and give up freedoms they'd otherwise hold sacred. Therefore George Orwell's political fiction resonates strongly because we all live in a time when our privacies are being eroded, while our governments assume more and more policies, "to keep us citizens safe." Making the novel 1984 more relevant than ever.

Big Brother is Watching You

Orwell set his story in a *dystopian* (not utopian) future where nuclear war had successfully divided the globe into three political realms or suppressive-super-states: Oceania, Eastasia, and Eurasia.

Orwell imagined the idea of an ever-watchful and ever-present Big Brother, (that could never be escaped). He foresaw the *Telescreen,* (a TV that observes those watching it). *Newspeak,* a form of speaking that totalitarian governments use to discourage free-thinking. He even saw the destruction of the family unit. As a result, such vocabulary as: *Double-think, Memory-hole, Thought-police* and the *Un-person,* have become part of popular culture.

He foresaw an outright ban on individuality and the persecution of free-thinkers (those who are *different* and *difficult* to indoctrinate), making non-conformity a major crime. So the popular idiom that developed, concerning life without freedom, became "BIG BROTHER IS WATCHING YOU!"

In his novel the *media* service was nothing more than a propaganda machine, and it's worth noting that George Orwell himself had worked with the BBC during World War II. During which time heavy restrictions existed, that limited what news could or could not be disseminated. Consequently he became greatly *disturbed* by what he perceived as the falseness of his work (fake news!)

To this degree Orwell had an up-close and first hand knowledge of the demands placed on journalists, to publicise falsehood, (best suiting whoever's in political power at any given time). Likewise it was Winston Smith, the novel's main character, who worked in the media and was responsible for creating deceptive propaganda. Actually, it's this, which gives Orwell's reader the best insight into the *duplicity* of the kind of society that he condemned the most.

Breaking the Matrix

Brexit created a real stir in recent times. British voters surprised the entire world because there's something about native Brits that non-natives will ever understand. You see we grew up singing proud anthems like: **"Rule Britannia. Britannia, rule the waves! Britons never, never, never shall be slaves."** This breeds a certain patriotic defiance that we are destined to rule but never be ruled - especially by BRUSSELS. Although times and political sentiments have changed much, these old-school sentiments have run deep through the tectonic layers of our culture and crossed generational lines.

The first verse of our National Anthem declares: "God save our gracious Queen, Long live our noble Queen, God save the Queen! Send her victorious, Happy and glorious, **Long to reign over us,** God save the Queen!" In other words, we're happy to be ruled by our *own* but not by any other.

Again, this sentiment runs deep in native Brits and is not to be underestimated, like it was during Brexit. If something is fed into the public psyche for generations - it cannot be erased in one political cycle. And as children, we were made aware of our outstanding history and influence upon the world stage at a very young age. It was something to be proud of. Just as American children were taught the Pledge of Allegiance and The Constitution etc.

Nowadays, there is little reverence for history with its monuments and statues either being defaced or torn down. (Globalists fuel this, because they want to do away with any vestiges or foundations from the past, so that they can form a new narrative - a progressive new order - that mustn't be contradicted by the past). In England we were raised on the notion of greatness - "GREAT BRITAIN" - ruler and coloniser of the world.

The Greatness went out of Britain a long time ago and while living in Germany for almost a decade, we discovered that lasting hostilities from the world wars still exist between our two nations. A certain disdain for the British still lingers, where we still get referred to as the "Island Monkeys!" Younger generations think much differently but it still trickles down.

However for native Britons, the act of capitulating to autocrats in Brussels is nothing short of an insult and a major blow to our national sense of pride, which in turn undermines our powerful legacy. A strong sense of indignation still resonates, something, which younger generations can't relate to.

So the distrust felt towards Brussels has been a long-held attitude and is not just a sudden mood swing. I can speak for the older generation who felt that British sovereignty was much more of a priority than immigration and yet the media said the opposite. I can confirm that most British people are not racist nor do they hate progress, again as the press tried to claim. **The tall and short of it is this; Brits are fiercely stubborn and independent people by nature. Brexit didn't shock those of us who understood that fact.**

This is purely on a human level though, without all the spiritual and prophetic implications involved, (which we won't go into here). I'll just say that the stage was set a long time ago.

On the subject of immigration however, most people we spoke to, voted to leave the EU because they just wanted to see common sense measures put in place, which would benefit everyone, including the immigrants. (People are not as dumb as the media makes out and can still think for themselves).

Common sense wasn't much to ask for right? So they made their voices heard and voted with their feet, on Thursday June 23, 2016 (in the United Kingdom European Union Membership Referendum) and the rest of the world is still in shock!

The EU Employs Orwellian Intelligence

So the Brits like to be in control of their own destiny and not give it away to Brussels. Their suspicions of the EU have not been hidden, for good reason. With this in mind, I refer to an article written by Ian Johnston from the Telegraph in 2009, concerning **public monitoring** in the EU, (if too controversial and Orwellian back then, how about today!)

The article reads in part: **"The EU is funding 'Orwellian' artificial intelligence to monitor the public... spending millions of pounds developing technologies designed to scour the Internet and CCTV images for 'abnormal behaviour'..."**[4]

Our question is, who gets to decide what's abnormal behaviour?

Then fast forward to 2017 and an article in the Guardian forewarned: **"Artificial intelligence is ripe for abuse, tech researcher warns: 'a fascist's dream.'** Microsoft's Kate Crawford tells SXSW that society must prepare for authoritarian movements to test the **'power without accountability'** of AI."[5]

It's a race for control, a power struggle. Those who control the world's intelligence (information) will literally rule the world. And the media play a huge role in this struggle for monopoly.

❖

CHAPTER 10

The Media & Artificial Intelligence in the End Times Part 2

There are many consequences to artificial intelligence and we are yet to find out the depth of them. **When Lady Diana died, the world mourned, then got angry.** Blaming the paparazzi (media) for causing her premature death and looking to profit from it. Her son, who was just 12 at the time of the incident, said the following during an interview with the BBC:

> One of the hardest things to come to terms with is the fact that the people who chased her into the tunnel were the same people who were taking photographs of her while she was still dying in the backseat of her car.
>
> **-- Prince Harry**

If the paparazzi have been intrusive in the past, (using zoom lenses as long as your arm), what about drone technology! There'll be no stopping them with their military level spying. How intrusive is it going to get? We've seen nothing yet. **Once they have the technology, they'll show zero restraint, just as they have proven time and time again (totally lacking any scruples).**

Another part of AI is Robo-Journalism:

You may not have realised how many types of journalism there are today but the list below (although inconclusive) gives you an idea of just how many different genres of journalism exist:

Adversarial journalism	Online journalism
Advocacy journalism	Parachute journalism
Ambush journalism	Participatory Media
Celebrity and people journalism	Political journalism
Citizen journalism	Robo-journalism
Comics journalism	Sensationalism
Community journalism	Service journalism
Convergence journalism	Science journalism
Data journalism	Sports journalism
Enterprise journalism	Social news
Environmental journalism	Solutions journalism

Fashion journalism	Trade journalism
Fake journalism	Unorthodox journalism
Geo-journalism	Video journalism
Innovation journalism	Video game journalism
Investigative journalism	Yellow journalism

Robo-journalism may be a new phenomenon for some people's ears but is fast becoming the norm. The following article explains:

"According to the *'infinite monkey theorem,'* a monkey randomly hitting keys on a typewriter for an infinite amount of time will almost certainly end up creating a literary masterpiece. Developments in artificial intelligence (AI) mean that AI can create a coherent written piece of text much quicker than that.

In fact, AI may be able to produce a news article in less time than a human can. With the increased demand for immediate news, there will be a surge in the deployment of AI to generate stories. However, as more of these 'robo-journalists' begin to 'create' news stories, legal issues relating to copyright, defamation, privacy and data protection arise.

AI is already being used to create news stories and reports. Natural language generation software powered AI has the ability to analyse data and quickly produce a story based on its analysis. Examples include 'Quill' developed by Narrative Science and 'Wordsmith' developed by Automated Insights."

Obviously some errors will still occur regardless and the article addresses this by saying: **"Though there will be legal issues under robo-journalists, it is worth bearing in mind that humans are also not perfect.** As long as media companies employ certain measures, e.g. appropriate quality control, transparency and/or a swift take down process, then **robo-journalism will become increasingly relied on as a source, particularly for types of news which rely on processing huge amounts of data very quickly, such as stories about financial and currency markets, sports results and weather data.**

With the increase in the Internet of things and data generally, the topics are likely to increase. **For these particular types of factual stories, human journalists may increasingly be replaced by technology."**

Journalists being, *replaced by technology*, is a credible eventuality, yet still there's plenty that technology hasn't mastered yet, which includes the complexities of humanity such as: emotions, individuality, personality and most of all wit and humour.

With this in mind, the article finishes by saying: **"However, it is hard to envisage AI replacing most other areas of journalism such as opinion pieces, humour, political analysis, human stories and the art of investigating and writing a breaking news piece, in the public interest, any time soon."**[1]

The Potential Misuse of Artificial Intelligence

AI without personality or humanity is one thing, but without accountability is another and is something that is troubling to many. Even some tech giants are beginning to grow a conscience.

According to the BBC: **"Google's Demis Hassabis warns that the misuse of artificial intelligence 'could do harm.' It is a technology so powerful that - on a distant day well into the future - it could mean computers that are able to advise on the best way to treat patients, tackle climate change or feed the poor. With such potential power, comes huge responsibility.**

Demis Hassabis, the head of Google's £400m machine learning business and one of the world's leading authorities on the subject, has now called for a responsible debate about the role of ethics in the development of artificial intelligence. **'I think artificial intelligence is like any powerful new technology,'** Mr Hassabis, DeepMind's co-founder, told me.

'It has to be used responsibly. If it's used irresponsibly it could do harm. I think we have to be aware of that and I think that people developing that - us and other companies and universities - need to realise and take seriously our responsibilities and to have ethical concerns at the top of our minds...

I think there are valid concerns and they should be discussed and debated now, decades before there's anything that's actually of any potential consequence or power that we need to worry about, so we have the answers in place well ahead of time.'

Mr Hassabis was responding to concerns about the development of artificial intelligence raised, among others, by Elon Musk, the technology entrepreneur and a DeepMind investor, and Professor Stephen Hawking. **Prof Hawking told my colleague Rory Cellan-Jones that artificial intelligence could 'end mankind.'**

AI - is the Science of making Machines Smart:

Mr Hassabis is not at the robots end of artificial intelligence. His work focuses on learning machines, which are able to sift huge amounts of data and support human understanding of the exponential rise of digitised information.

'Artificial intelligence is the science of making machines smart,' he said. 'If we're able to imbue machines with intelligence then they might be able to help us as a society to solve all kinds of big problems that we would like to have a better mastery of - all the way from things like disease and healthcare, to big questions we have in science like climate change and physics, **where having the ability for machines to understand and find insights in large amounts of data could be very helpful to the human scientists and doctors.'**

His world is a long way from Hollywood's take on artificial intelligence. Terminator or the beguiling Ava in Ex Machina might make for 'good entertainment' but the world is fanciful. Computers, Mr Hassabis says, are nowhere near being able to ape human behaviour or over take human thinking. Terminator is one of those examples that is very iconic, but extremely unrealistic in a number of ways."

Who Controls or Regulates the Machines?

Finally he says, "'Certainly that's not what I worry about, it's more where there are unintended things - something you might have missed, rather than people intentionally building systems to control weapons and other things.' **And this touches on the knotty subject of regulation... 'I think it's much too early to think about regulation,'** Mr Hassabis said."

Evidently then, just as there was major uncertainty about how to regulate the Internet, the same is true of artificial intelligence. (In fact net-neutrality has been a very controversial issue going into 2018).

BBC's Business Editor Kamel Ahmed said, "We're very early in this technology phase, **so we don't really know yet what the right things would be to regulate...** But unlike in the past - where we were also there at the dawn of the computer age and yet Silicon Valley ended up doing all the innovation and reaping most of the commercial benefits - we should make sure that we stay at the forefront of what will be an incredibly important technology in the next 10 or 20 years. **By then, society may well need answers to the question - who controls the machines?"**[2]

Anaesthetised to the Risks

Personally, we think it's already high time to ask who controls these machines? Is there a good reason not to? **Yet we've been quickly anaesthetised to the risks of artificial intelligence, mostly due to cultural osmosis, via social media and the entertainment industry.**

In England we had "Big Brother 2000," (also referred to as Big-Brother-One), which was the first series of the British reality television show Big Brother. It was designed first to shock; then to normalise (crass and crude behaviour) so that we grew *indifferent* to the idea of being "watched" 24/7.

Entertainment is so powerful because it influences us while our guard is low. Nothing shocks us anymore and Facebook in particular has used our own narcissistic tendencies against us. We don't realise how vulnerable we have become, which is entirely self-inflicted. **And the ultimate irony of social media is that we regularly share our personal information with complete strangers from around the world, but don't even talk to our next-door neighbours!**

What the Tech Giants Think of AI

Normalizing AI through entertainment is a clever tactic aimed at eliminating any associated fears that are attached to this form of progressive technology.

Some of the biggest names in tech right now, such as **Elon Musk, Mark Cuban and Mark Zuckerberg** – are trying to get ahead of the curve particularly where AI is concerned. Two of which are said to be interested in politics. Which sparked my interest in Mark Cuban for instance, the multi billionaire who just announced that he is "actively considering" running for president in 2020, against Donald Trump.

What struck me as remarkable was his admission of fear towards AI or rather his healthy reverence towards it. He said in an interview that he was learning as much about artificial intelligence as he possibly could, and as fast as he could because of the pace that the industry is moving. And why my attention was pricked is because, politics (with its penchant for corruption) and AI make a real potent mix.

We don't take an alarmist approach to this, but it doesn't take a scientist to recognise that super-surveillance in the wrong hands spells big trouble - Orwellian by design. Mr Cuban and Mr Musk in particular are both smart enough to grasp what's really at stake and both air on the side of caution, while the much younger Mr Zuckerberg is giddy by comparison.

Tesla, Cuban and Zuckerberg:

The reason that these three tech giants are pivotal and that their opinions count is that one influences the other. Read the following:

"Tesla and SpaceX CEO Elon Musk may sound like an alarmist when he talks about the threat that artificial intelligence (AI) poses to humans, but he's got an ally in billionaire Mark Cuban, owner of the basketball team Dallas Mavericks and a lead investor on *Shark Tank*. On Sunday at New York City's OZY FEST, **Cuban had similarly drastic language about the advancements in machine learning that are coming and even happening now; he said that AI is already 'changing everything.'**

His opinions are not unlike those of Elon Musk, who called AI a **'fundamental risk to the existence of human civilization'** at the National Governors Association meeting this month. **Musk advocated for governmental regulation of AI, saying that a forthcoming massive replacement of human employees is the biggest threat AI poses to global society.**

Cuban thinks that these changes are already occurring. **'Without question, machine learning, computer vision and neural networks are changing everything,'** Cuban said. 'However much change you saw over the past ten years with the Apple iPhone, that's nothing.'

Cuban has sounded the alarm in the past, too. In February, he said that **any person who doesn't learn about AI is 'going to be a dinosaur within 3 years,'** and again cautioned that major job losses will soon occur."[3]

They Agree to disagree about the dangers of Under-estimating AI:

"Multi-billionaire tech titan... Mark Cuban says that **most people are underestimating the potential of artificial intelligence to change the world we live and work in.** He's especially intimidated, by the pace at which new technology advances: 'It scares the s--- out of me,' says Cuban, speaking to Ozy Fest conference attendees in New York City. **'However much change you saw over the last 10 years with the iPhone, over the last 20 years with the Internet, over the last 30 years with PC's, etc., that is nothing. Nothing!'** Cuban says.

'Things are getting faster, processing is getting faster, machines are starting to think,' he continues. **'And either**

you make them think for you or they will take your place and do the thinking for you.'"[4]

So does all this amount to fear, control or be controlled, or is it a genuine warning from those who've had high-level exposure, to never underestimate artificial intelligence.

According to CNBC, "SpaceX and Tesla CEO Elon Musk says the potential is frightening. **'I have exposure to the most cutting edge AI, and I think people should be really concerned by it,' Musk said earlier in July (2017). 'AI is a fundamental risk to the existence of human civilization.'**

Meanwhile, Facebook CEO and billionaire Mark Zuckerberg says AI will make our lives better and safer. **'With AI especially, I am really optimistic,' says Zuckerberg. 'I think people who are naysayers and try to drum up these doomsday scenarios — I just, I don't understand it. It's really negative and in some ways I actually think it is pretty irresponsible.'** Musk counters that the CEO of Facebook's 'understanding of the subject is limited.'

As the tech elite argue over the potential implications, Cuban says the U.S. is losing ground in the innovation race. 'Montreal and Vancouver and Toronto are just kicking our a-- in artificial intelligence. So is China,' he says."[5]

There you have it, the tech giants and elites of Silicon Valley are racing to get ahead of the curve. Artificial intelligence appears to be the ultimate information gateway that's now trying to control the earth; from artificial neural networks, intelligent appliances and smart phones, just to name a few.

But let me end this chapter by saying that Satan is a control freak. How better to attempt to control the inhabitants of earth than through technology? He's not omniscient, omnipotent or omnipresent. He is not deity. BUT he tries. And through technology can attempt to possess humanity.

We must understand that Satan doesn't want to possess our smart devises, such as toasters, fridge or iPhones! He's not even interested in our cars or jobs; he is after our MINDS and must resort to technology like AI in order to achieve it.

We need discernment in these end times, **"Lest Satan should get an advantage of us: for we are not ignorant of his devices"** (2 Corinthians 2:11 KJV).

❖

CHAPTER 11

The Global Phenomena
of Facebook & Social Media

Zuck for President? According to Vox, "If you read media coverage of Mark Zuckerberg's national tour, it's easy to get the impression that the Facebook billionaire is running for president. But Zuckerberg says he's not running for office. He says he simply wants to get to know Americans — most of whom are Facebook users — better."

A Corporate Goodwill Tour or Presidential Campaign?

"A lot of people think Zuckerberg is preparing for a possible presidential run. Zuck himself denies it, insisting that he's just trying to get to know the country — and, importantly, American Facebook users — better...

As the CEO of one of the world's most influential companies, Zuckerberg has a lot of the same concerns. Most Americans are Facebook users, so almost every meeting Zuckerberg has helps him understand Facebook users better. And if he can make himself well-liked by the public, that public goodwill will make it easier for Facebook to weather future controversies.

And that's important because it's practically guaranteed that a company of Facebook's size and influence will eventually come under public scrutiny. Already, the company has faced criticism (from Vox and others) for the proliferation of fake news on its platform, and people have blasted Facebook for doing too little to scrub violent videos from the site...

Hubbard argues that Zuckerberg woke up after Donald Trump's election and realized that he didn't understand American Facebook users as well as he thought he did. Critics charged that Facebook had facilitated the spread of fake news that may have contributed to Trump's victory.

So, Hubbard says, Zuckerberg has 'ventured out into the world beyond his bubble to do field research.' He's trying to meet as many Facebook users as possible — from as many backgrounds as possible — **to help shape his thinking as he considers how to *improve* Facebook in the next few years."**[1]

How Facebook Censors
Christians and Conservatives

What exactly does, ***"improve* Facebook in the next few years"** really mean? Perhaps it's referring to the systematic singling-out and silencing of conservatives who express their Judeo-Christian values and ideology. The question then has to be, is this the beginning of censorship for Christians? The next segment shows the beginning of open persecution on Facebook. My wife has often said, "The modern Coliseum - as a venue to persecute Christians - is the Internet."

A standard dictionary definition of censorship:
"The suppression or prohibition of any parts of books, films, news, etc. that are considered obscene, politically unacceptable, or a threat to security."

Diamond and Silk:

Take this for example, early in 2018 YouTube sparked outrage by allegedly censoring a popular conservative duo from the United States. The two African-American Trump supporters, Lynnette Hardaway and Rochelle Richardson, aka Diamond and Silk, accused YouTube of outright *censorship,* and the violation of their 1st Amendment rights. This came after the company demonetised 95% of their videos.

The pair rose to fame during the 2016 election for their no-nonsense-delivery and entertaining videos - in support of Mr Trump.

Several online sources claimed that the company's treatment of the pair was part of an overall CRACK DOWN to silence Trump Supporters specifically.

Not only Google and YouTube but Facebook too, as Ethan Huff of Natural News.com reported, "Late last year

[2016], Facebook announced its own fight against then-candidate Donald Trump, reportedly pushing its employees to remove all pro-Trump content from the platform as if it was *hate speech*. The Wall Street Journal (WSJ) reported that **Facebook CEO Mark Zuckerberg later relented, admitting that such censorship would be *'inappropriate.'"*[2]

Casualties of YouTube's attempt to Silence Extremism:

The Washington Times quoted the pair from a series of their tweets saying, "Wonder if @YouTube @TeamYouTube stopped the monetization of our videos because we are loyal supporters of the @POTUS. Hummmm. Sounds like Censorship to us, which is a Violation of our First Amendment. A Bias Method used to Silence our Conservative Voices. **@YouTube, how was it OK to monetize our videos for the past two years and now those same videos are no longer eligible for monetization?"**

With 89,000 subscribers on YouTube and another 361,000 on Twitter, this news provoked a stir, with the online sensations openly alleging that their videos had become "casualties of the company's attempt to silence *extremism.*"

This comes after the company announced [in Aug 2017] plans to fight inappropriate content, **"We'll soon be applying tougher treatment to videos that aren't illegal but have been flagged by users as potential violations of our policies on hate speech and violent extremism...** If we find that these videos don't violate our policies but contain controversial religious or supremacist content, they will be placed in a limited state. The videos will remain on YouTube behind an interstitial, won't be recommended, won't be monetized, and won't have key features including comments, suggested videos, and likes."[3]

Felix Ngole:

However back in 2015, Felix Ngole wrote on his personal Facebook page that "same sex marriage is a sin whether we like it or not. It is God's words and man's sentiments would not change His words... the Bible and God identify homosexuality as a sin."

Controversial? Sure. But he still had a right to express his own thoughts on his "personal" Facebook page right? Well, one would assume so but the real answer to this was a resounding, "No."

According to CBN Christian Broadcasting Network: "A UK court has ruled that a university's decision to expel a Christian student over his comments on homosexuality is legal... Ngole, who was studying social work at Sheffield University, was immediately expelled for the comments. However the 39-year-old student challenged the university's decision arguing that expelling him was a breach of his human rights."

Freedom of Speech, Religion and Human Rights:

Officials from Sheffield University had a different view, saying that while Ngole, "was fully entitled to his religious beliefs, and had acted with honesty and integrity," it was his decision to make his views public that was in question. They argued that he **"may have caused offence to some**

individuals." Which begs the question, what about all the other content on Facebook that *may cause offence to some individuals?*

"A UK court agreed with the university's position, claiming Ngole's public comments on homosexuality 'could be accessed and read by people who would perceive them as judgmental, incompatible with service ethos, or suggestive of discriminatory intent.'

'That was a problem in its own right,' the court ruled. 'But whatever the actual intention was, it was the perception of the posting that would cause the damage. **It was reasonable to be concerned about that perception.'"**

Okay then let me ask, if universities and big businesses are so concerned about *perceptions,* then what about the perceptions and opinions of Christians, don't they count as well? And how many Facebook users are Christian anyways, isn't Mark Zuckerberg afraid of offending them too?

While he continues to fight the discrimination Ngole said, "To me it sends a chilling message that **if you are a Christian and you hold traditional Christian views you should be careful not to express them** because you might end up losing your job."

Over time, we've personally witnessed the societal metamorphosis of Britain, where it has become increasingly anti-Christian, through capitulation to things like Sharia law for example and through embracing other cultures, to the point that they openly vy for supremacy over its Judeo-Christian values and traditions.

Freedom to believe without Freedom of Expression is no Freedom at All:

So when it comes to human rights, are we as a society, becoming a little too selective about whose rights we are actually protecting? What about all the porn that gets onto Facebook? What about those women's rights? Of course that's just one obvious example but there are many.

Sadly Facebook's double standards are increasingly blatant and deliberate. Is this all part of the "improvements" that Mr Zuckerberg wants to make? Time will reveal just how far Facebook is willing to go in its anti-Christian policy, considering just how many Christians use Facebook to network globally, which is something that Mr Zuckerberg is not blind to.

Andrea Williams, chief executive of the Christian Legal Centre, who represented Mr Ngole released the following statement:

"The court has ruled that though Mr Ngole is entitled to hold his Biblical views on sexual ethics, he is not entitled to express them. **But freedom to believe without freedom of expression is no freedom at all."**

Which just about says it all. However she continued:

"Many views are frequently expressed by students on social media and in other contexts. **It is the expression of Biblical morality that has been singled out for sanction by the university.** This ruling will have a chilling effect on Christian students up and down the country who will now understand that their **personal social media posts may be investigated for political correctness...** Rulings like this show that society is becoming increasingly intolerant of Christian moral values. Christians are being told to shut up and keep quiet about their moral views or face a bar from employment."

Ngole concludes with, "I intend to appeal this decision which clearly intends to restrict me from expressing my Christian faith in public... Unless the views you express are politically correct, you may be barred from office. This is very far from how a free and fair society should operate."[4]

Changing Society & Exploiting a Vulnerability in Human Psychology

God only knows what it's doing to our children's brains.

-- Sean Parker

Ex-Facebook president and billionaire Sean Parker says that creators knew that Facebook (and social media in general) would be damaging for the future and create untold ramifications. **He claims that it was purposefully created to exploit human vulnerability.**

Facebook's Original Mission was to Trap us in its Tentacles:

"In an interview with Axios' Mike Allen, Parker, who was portrayed in the movie 'The Social Network' by Justin Timberlake said, **'Social networks have the power now to alter society and not for the better.'**

Parker was the company's first president and is now the founder and chair of the Parker Institute for Cancer Immunotherapy. He made the comments at an event to discuss accelerating innovation for cancer therapies.

The 37-year-old billionaire, who is also known for having founded the file-sharing network Napster in the late 1990s, added that **Facebook's mission in the early days was just about getting you hooked into its tentacles...**

Others feel the same:

Parker, who has a net worth of over $2 billion, is not the only former Facebook employee to feel as if the company may be doing more harm than good. The creator of the 'like' button, former Facebook engineer Justin Rosenstein, said he thinks his invention is a contributor to 'time poorly spent.'

But not Mark:

Zuckerberg, who has asked for 'forgiveness' for ways his 'work was used to divide people,' revealed Facebook's new mission statement this past summer. In June [2017], the 31-year-old Zuckerberg said the company's new purpose is **'to give people the power to build community and bring the world closer together.'"**[5]

Conscientious Objector

According to another source concerning the same interview, Mike Allen is quoted as saying, **"Sean Parker... gave me a candid insider's look at how social networks purposely hook and potentially hurt our brains.** Parker's

I-was-there account provides priceless perspective in the rising debate about the power and effects of the social networks, which now have scale and reach unknown in human history. He's worried enough that he's sounding the alarm...

In the green room, Parker mentioned that he has become **'something of a conscientious objector' on social media.** By the time he left the stage, he jokingly said Mark Zuckerberg will probably block his account after reading this:

- When Facebook was getting going, I had these people who would come up to me and they would say, 'I'm not on social media.' And I would say, 'OK. You know, you will be.' And then they would say, 'No, no, no. I value my real-life interactions. I value the moment. I value presence. I value intimacy.' And I would say, ... **'We'll get you eventually.'**

- I don't know if I really understood the consequences of what I was saying, because [of] the unintended consequences of a network when it grows to a billion or 2 billion people and ... **it literally changes your relationship with society, with each other ... It probably interferes with productivity in weird ways. God only knows what it's doing to our children's brains.**

- The thought process that went into building these applications, Facebook being the first of them, ... was all about: **'How do we consume as much of your time and conscious attention as possible?'**

- And that means that we need to sort of give you a little dopamine hit every once in a while, because someone liked or commented on a photo or a post or whatever. And that's going to get you to contribute more content, and that's going to get you ... more likes and comments.

- It's a social-validation feedback loop ... exactly the kind of thing that a hacker like myself would come up with, because you're **exploiting a vulnerability in human psychology.**

- **The inventors, creators** — it's me, it's Mark [Zuckerberg], it's Kevin Systrom on Instagram, it's all of these people — **understood this consciously. And we did it anyway."**[6]

Though the science is still coming in, all the evidence is pointing to the facts that suggest Facebook is bad for your health, your children's brains, your marriage, your expectations of life and last but not least your emotional equilibrium. So let's see what those in the medical profession are saying.

❖

CHAPTER 12

What the Psychologists are Saying about Facebook

Aaccording to author and psychologist Douglas Kenrick, "Facebook's meteoric rise in popularity suggests that it offers us something we've always wanted... But like all benefits in life, **Facebook comes with its psychological costs — many of them invisible. Indeed, a recent study found that heavy Facebook users experience decreases in subjective well-being over time** (Kross et al., 2013). Below we review some research suggesting 7 ways that Facebook may be hurting you.

7 Ways Facebook is bad for your Mental Health:
(How staying in-touch may be driving you nuts)

1. **It can make you feel like your life isn't as cool as everyone else's:**

   Social psychologist Leon Festinger observed that people are naturally inclined to engage in social comparison. To answer a question like 'Am I doing better or worse than average?' you need to check out other people like you. Facebook is a quick, effortless way to engage in social comparison, but with even one glance through your News Feed you might see pictures of your friends enjoying a mouth-watering dinner at Chez Panisse, or perhaps winning the Professor of the Year award at Yale University. Indeed, a study by Chou and Edge (2012) found that chronic Facebook users tend to think that other people lead happier lives than their own, leading them to feel that life is less fair.

2. **It can lead you to envy your friends' successes:**

   Did cousin Annabelle announce a nice new promotion last month, a new car last week, and send a photo from her cruise vacation to Aruba this morning? Not only can Facebook make you feel like you aren't sharing in your friends' happiness, but it can also make you feel envious of their happy lives. Buxmann and Krasnova (2013) have found that seeing others' highlights on your News Feed can make you envious of friends' travels, successes, and appearances. Additional findings suggest that the negative psychological impact of passively following others on Facebook is driven by the feelings of envy that stem from passively skimming your News Feed.

3. **It can lead to a sense of false consensus:**

   Sit next to a friend while you each search for the same thing on Google. Eli Pariser, author of *The Filter Bubble* (2012), can promise you won't see the same search results. Not only have your Internet searches grown more personalized, so have social networking sites. Facebook's sorting function places posts higher in your News Feed if they're from like-minded friends — which may distort your view of the world (Constine, 2012). This can lead you to believe that your favourite political candidate is a shoe-in for the upcoming election, even though many of your friends are saying otherwise...you just won't hear them.

4. **It can keep you in touch with people you'd really rather forget:**

   Want to know what your ex is up to? You can...and that might not be a good thing. Facebook stalking has made it harder to let go of past relationships. Does she seem as miserable as I am? Is that ambiguous post directed at me? Has she started dating that guy from trivia night? These questions might better remain unanswered; indeed, Marshall (2012) found that Facebook users who reported visiting their former partner's page experienced disrupted post-breakup emotional recovery and higher levels of distress. Even if you still run into your ex in daily life, the effects of online surveillance were significantly worse than those of offline contact.

5. **It can make you jealous of your current partner:**

Facebook stalking doesn't only apply to your ex. Who is this Stacy LaRue, and why is she constantly 'liking' my husband's Facebook posts? Krafsky and Krafsky, authors of *Facebook and Your Marriage* (2010), address many common concerns in relationships that stem from Facebook use. 'Checking up on' your partner's page can often lead to jealousy and even unwarranted suspicion, particularly if your husband's exes frequently come into the picture. Krafsky and Krafsky recommend talking with your partner about behaviors that you both consider safe and trustworthy on Facebook, and setting boundaries where you don't feel comfortable.

6. **It can reveal information you might not want to share with potential employers:**

Do you really want a potential employer to know about how drunk you got at last week's kegger...or the interesting wild night that followed with the girl in the blue bikini? Peluchette and Karl (2010) found that 40% of users mention alcohol use on their Facebook page, and 20% mention sexual activities. We often think these posts are safe from prying eyes, but that might not be the case. While 89% of jobseekers use social networking sites, 37% of potential employers do, as well — and are actively looking into their potential hires (Smith, 2013). If you're on the job market, make sure to check your privacy settings and restrict any risqué content to 'Friends Only,' if you don't wish to delete it entirely.

7. **It can become addictive:**

Think society's most common addictive substances are coffee, cigarettes, and alcohol? Think again. The DSM-V (Diagnostic and Statistical Manual) includes a new diagnosis that has stirred controversy: a series of items gauging Internet Addiction. Since then, Facebook addiction has gathered attention from both popular media and empirical journals, leading to the creation of a Facebook addiction scale (Paddock, 2012). To explore the seriousness of this addiction, Hofmann and colleagues (2012) randomly texted participants over the course of a week to ask what they most desired at that particular moment. They found that among their participants, social media use was craved even more than tobacco and alcohol.

Of course, the news isn't all that bad. Some research finds Facebook may decrease loneliness when used to keep up to date—and keep in touch with—others. Fenne Deters and Matthias Mehl (2012) randomly assigned participants to post more status updates than they typically did per week, and found that this led to increased feelings of social connectedness, and lower levels of loneliness. In the end, Facebook is probably a lot like other technological advances, such as the automobile – whether or not it hurts you or cousin Annabelle, depends on where y'all drive and how frequently y'all get behind the wheel."[1]

"Facebook-Depression" is Really a Thing:

So the consensus is continually growing and according to **Forbes,** "The American Academy of Paediatrics has warned about the potential for negative effects of social media in young kids and teens, including **cyber-bullying and 'Facebook depression.'**

Social media isn't very good for mental well-being, and in some ways, it can be pretty damaging... This is not to say that there's *no* benefit to social media — obviously it keeps us connected across great distances, and helps us find people we'd lost touch with years ago. But getting on social when you have some time to kill, or, worse, need an emotional lift, is very likely a bad idea. And studies have found that taking a break from Facebook helps boost psychological well-being."[2]

According to the BBC, Internet psychologist Graham Jones, member of the British Psychological Society says, "Studies have found - there is a growing depth of research that suggests Facebook has negative consequences."[3]

Facebook's Dark-Side
A platform for Multiple Disorders

Let's go a little deeper. More recently researchers have established a direct link between Facebook and what is considered **"socially disruptive narcissism"** - the most toxic elements of narcissistic personality disorder.

Grandiose Exhibitionism & Entitlement/Exploitativeness:

"Researchers at Western Illinois University studied the Facebook habits of 294 students, aged between 18 and 65, and measured two 'socially disruptive' elements of narcissism – **Grandiose Exhibitionism (GE) and Entitlement/ Exploitativeness (EE).**

GE includes: 'self-absorption, vanity, superiority, and exhibitionistic tendencies' and people who score high on this aspect of narcissism need to be constantly at the centre of attention. They often say shocking things and inappropriately self-disclose because they cannot stand to be ignored or waste a chance of self-promotion.

The EE aspect includes: 'a sense of deserving respect and a willingness to manipulate and take advantage of others.'

Excessive Self-Promotion:

The research revealed that the higher someone scored on aspects of GE, the greater the number of friends they had on Facebook, with some amassing more than 800. Those scoring highly on EE and GE were also more likely to accept friend requests from strangers and seek social support, but less likely to provide it, according to the research.

Carol Craig, a social scientist and chief executive of the Centre for Confidence and Well-being, said **young people in Britain were becoming increasingly narcissistic and Facebook provided a platform for the disorder.**

'The way that children are being educated is focussing more and more on the importance of self esteem – on how you are seen in the eyes of others. This method of teaching has been imported from the US and is *all-about-me.* Facebook provides a platform for people to self-promote by changing profile pictures and showing how many hundreds of friends you have...'

Damaged Egos seek Social Support on Facebook:

Dr Viv Vignoles, senior lecturer in social psychology at Sussex University, said there was 'clear evidence' from studies in America that college students were becoming increasingly narcissistic.

But he added: 'Whether the same is true of non-college students or of young people in other countries, such as the UK, remains an open question, as far as I know. Without understanding the causes underlying the historical change in US college students, we do not know whether these causes are factors that are relatively specific to American culture, such as the political focus on increasing self-esteem in the late 80s and early 90s or whether they are factors that are more general, for example new technologies such as mobile phones and Facebook.'

Vignoles said, 'The correlational nature of the latest study meant it was difficult to be certain whether individual differences in narcissism led to certain patterns of Facebook behaviour, whether patterns of Facebook behaviour led to individual differences in narcissism, or a bit of both.'

Christopher Carpenter, who ran the study, said: 'In general, the *dark side* of Facebook requires more research in order to better understand Facebook's socially beneficial and harmful aspects in order to enhance the former and curtail the latter.

If Facebook is to be a place where people go to repair their damaged ego and seek social support, it is vitally important to discover the potentially negative communication one might find on Facebook and the kinds of people likely to engage in them. **Ideally, people will engage in pro-social Facebooking rather than anti-social me-booking.'"**[4]

Twitter & Trump Unfiltered

Though we don't want to linger here, we couldn't talk about media without mentioning the twitter-sphere or twitter-verse that hosts President Donald Trump as a perpetual user; by which his freedom of speech is being exercised - at the complete grievance and annoyance of the liberal media who cannot control the flow of information that Mr Trump spews! They try very hard to distort and delay but ultimately can't stop Mr Trump from tweeting. Endless mocking clearly doesn't work.

Something else peaked my interest however that reveals more about the President than most other things. One of his closest aids, Daniel Scavino Jr. officially called the White House's Director of Social Media, once used to be his golf caddy! On first hearing, it's a heart-warming story that includes humility, respect and most of all loyalty.

President Trump has been strongly criticised for his usage of Twitter and social media and for not being presidential. Much space and time has been given to this debate. We're not joining that here. But what interests us more is that Dan Scavino was just 16 years old when he first met Donald Trump who told him, "You'll work for me someday, in a big way." Now in his early 40's he enjoys close proximity to the President and his family; running the on-going social media campaign. He has the responsibility of getting the President's message out there free and unfiltered by the press. Loyalty pays off.

Notice - how all the negative press only causes a rallying-effect? The more negative the press, the more people rally to defend the President (besides the media). Those who see through all the media attacks, because they are far too frequent and bias to be fair. It's a good thing that many who would normally be passively-aggressive towards politics on the whole, are now far more willing and passionate to defend someone who is being unfairly treated.

So be encouraged, what the enemy intends for harm is conversely having a positive effect instead. The public – on all sides of the debate are becoming far more accountable for their political views. They have to know where they stand or don't. The lines are being drawn, creating a sharper contrast between right and wrong, light and dark, night and day (an unavoidable consequence of these end days).

BUT who knew it would take someone like DONALD J. TRUMP, with the courage to stand up to the political and religious status quo, to show everyone else how to "take-the-heat." He's taken everyone to school. Who knew!

❖

CHAPTER 13

Google
The Largest Country
in the World

We're always on the look out for interesting articles, interviews or books and this particular book caught our attention recently after watching an interview with author Scott Cleland, **"Search & Destroy: Why You Can't Trust Google Inc."** It was just what we were looking for.

The interview with Scott was interesting to say the least and although he's already widely published, Scott is considered a leading Google critic; testifying before Congress (three times) specifically about Google and is a former U.S. Deputy Assistant Secretary of State for Information and

Communication Policy. Making him a firm authority on the subject.

In an earlier chapter of this book, we already covered what is means for a society to become "Orwellian." One characteristic in particular was *duplicity,* which describes the behaviour of some governments and the media, when attempting to control mass information. **According to Scott there is none guiltier of duplicity than Google!**

Master of Duplicity

In his book Scott holds nothing back and reveals how the world's most powerful company is not who it pretends to be, a benign and benevolent *manager,* who helps us organise our lives.

Instead he warns us, "Google has acquired far more information, both public and private, and has invented more ways to use it, than anyone in history. **Information is power, and in Google's case, it is the power to influence and control virtually everything the Internet touches."**

He goes on, **"Google's power is largely unchecked, unaccountable, and grossly underestimated. Google is the Internet's lone superpower, the new master of the digital information universe. And Google's power depends almost entirely on the blind trust it has gained through masterful duplicity. Google routinely says one thing and does another."**

In the interview Scott went on to talk about how this world number one brand is completely untrustworthy and unethical as it hides behind the **"Don't be Evil"** slogan with its hidden political agendas. Revealing just how Google's famed mission to **"organize the world's information"** was and is utterly destructive and deeply immoral, considering where Google is leading us.

"Google's centralization of power over the world's information is corrupting both Google and the Internet, which is a natural result of unchecked power. Google is evolving from an information servant to master, from working for users, to making users work for the Internet behemoth…

Google's goal is to change the world by influencing and controlling information access. Ultimately, Google's immense unchecked power is destructive precisely because Google is so political, unethical and untrustworthy."

Destroying Privacy and Individualism:

Considering how George Orwell perceived the future, he was pretty spot-on. One particular concern he had was about world governments and the media's outright attack on individuality. According to Scott, **"Google's pervasive tracking and profiling destroys privacy and individualism and uses its 'Don't be Evil' slogan to mask unethical business practices."**

Scott further warned, "Google's market dominance and free products threaten competition, innovation, job creation, and economic growth. Its hidden political agenda threatens individual freedom, democracy, and national sovereignty." Mostly Scott's deepest concerns rested with, "the ramifications of Google imposing its radical values and ideology on the world."[1]

EU hits Google with a Record Anti-trust Fine of $2.7 Billion:

According to an article on CNBC, "EU regulators fined Google a record 2.4 billion euros ($2.7 billion) Tuesday, ruling that the search-engine giant violated anti-trust rules for its online shopping practices. The fine is the largest doled out by Brussels for a monopoly abuse case and follows a seven-year-long investigation.

'Google has abused its dominance as a search engine by giving illegal advantages to another Google product, its shopping comparison service,' Commissioner Margrethe Vestager told reporters.

Investigations were triggered after the European Commission received dozens of complaints from U.S. and European competitors who claimed that the company abused its search market dominance to give its Google Shopping service an advantage over other retailers and create a monopoly over consumers.

Though the company was charged with distorting Internet results by the EU competition authority in April 2015 it has not before faced fines for an abuse of this nature and marks a landmark for the way technology companies are regulated. The business has been given 90 days to cease these practices or face further penalties. This may include noncompliance payments of up to 5 percent of Google parent

Alphabet's daily worldwide turnover. **Google will consider appealing.**"[2]

Unelected and Unregulated

Google should be regulated like the public utility it is.

-- **Tucker Carlson**

The Public Ridicule and Open Example made of James Damore:

At the end of 2017, the left-leaning Google, very publically dismissed one of its own software engineers named James Damore. Author of a 10-page essay (approx.), which subsequently went viral, calling for a political-culture-change at the company: "We need to stop assuming that gender gaps imply sexism," he wrote.

Now widely documented, Google's newly minted Vice President of Diversity, Integrity and Governance, Danielle Brown, released a statement saying that Damore had, "incorrect assumptions about gender." She didn't expand on this however, because no one in the media was asking!

In fact nearly all the news organizations described the essay as, **an anti-diversity memo** when actually it was ultimately suggesting that Google's inner culture required more diversity. In reaction to this exemplary dismissal Carlson said, **"In perhaps the most Orwellian statement written since Orwell himself finished 1984, Google explained the firing: 'Part of building an open and inclusive environment means fostering a culture in which those with alternative** views, including different political views, feel safe sharing their opinions.'"

Refuting it further Carlson went on to say, "Okay. So in order to foster a culture in which those with alternative political views could feel safe sharing their opinions, **Google fired James Damore for the crime of sharing his alternative political opinions. Huh! At no point, did Google rebut any of the points Damore made, the fact he made them was enough. <u>Raising questions was his crime.</u>**

Now, why does any of this matter? **Well, it matters because Google is the most powerful company in the history of the world. <u>It's the portal through which the bulk of our information flows</u>. That means that if Google isn't on the level, neither is our understanding of the world. To an unprecedented extent, <u>Google controls reality</u>. Now Google has already shown a disturbing willingness to distort reality for ideological ends,"** he concluded.

Who voted Google as Ruler of the World?

So this is the bizarre reality we all now live in, regardless which country we dwell in. Google has no country, no allegiances and no boundaries. **Google is Google and essentially controls all of us.** Just one example of this is when Google was sued back in 2008 for refusing to allow anti-abortion advertisements on its platforms even while freely allowing pro-abortion ones.

Now Google has appointed itself as the world's online judge and jury of fake news by changing its search algorithms

120

so that what it considers fake news won't even show up in our searches. It will be as invisible as if it didn't exist at all! This means that Google gets to decide what's offensive or fake. That's the dangerous part.

We know that this self-appointed Guardian of Truth cannot be trusted and has been willing to shut down free speech for political reasons with the power to dictate what the world sees, thinks and knows. **All of this power without ever being elected into office! Who voted for Google to rule the world?**

With too much power Google has already suffered some consequences for violating anti-trust laws here in Europe, yet still it seeks to censor the Internet, whether we like it or not.

We agree; Google needs to be regulated like any other public utility to ensure it doesn't continue distorting the free flow of global information.

❖

CHAPTER 14

Socialism
Creating the Ultimate
Safe-Space

According to the Merriam Webster Dictionary the Definition of Socialism is: "Any of various economic and political theories advocating collective or governmental ownership and administration of the means of production and distribution of goods.

A system of society or group living in which there is no private property. A system or condition of society in which the means of production are owned and controlled by the state. A stage of society in Marxist theory transitional between capitalism and communism and distinguished by unequal distribution of goods and pay according to work done."[1]

If socialism were effective, then countries like North Korea, Russia and Cuba would be literal paradises on the earth right now – proven utopias! But we all know that history confirms otherwise.

National socialism tries to make history without God.
-- Prophesied by the late Kim Clement in 2010

Studies show Millennials Prefer Socialism to Capitalism:

Millennials are turned on to socialism, even with the most recent failure of Venezuela - to prove the point - with its socialist government on the verge of collapse for the past year (2017). Poor Venezuelans often struggle to find the basics, like food and other staple goods such as toilet paper! They are losing weight and being humiliated on the global stage.

Unless millennials feel they're able to put a totally modern spin on socialism, they're either deeply naïve or totally misguided. Yet many of them are persuaded that capitalism with its "trickle-down-economics" in particular, hasn't worked for their parents, so why would it work for them. Which is why out-spoken political figures like Jeremy Corbyn of the UK and Bernie Saunders in the US are popular today. Although both figures are notably older, they have certain appeal amongst the younger generations.

Widespread Historical Illiteracy:

Millennials are often branded as "misinformed" and "ignorant" concerning socialism and communism, despite being the most educated generation in history.

"Millennials think socialism would create a great safe space, study finds. Nearly half of all U.S. millennials believe the greatest safe space of them all would be living under a socialist regime.

That's according to a new study from research firm YouGov and Washington, D.C.-based Victims of Communism Memorial Foundation, which surveyed over 2,000 people regarding their views on socialism and the communist political system. The biggest takeaway from the study was that **one out of every two millennials surveyed said they would rather live in a socialist or communist country over a capitalist democracy like the U.S.**

'Millennials now make up the largest generation in America, and we're seeing some deeply worrisome trends,' Marion Smith, executive director of the foundation said in a statement to Fox News. 'Millennials are increasingly turning away from capitalism and toward socialism and even communism as a viable alternative.'

Nearly 45 percent of millennials polled said that they would prefer to live in a socialist country compared to the 42 percent who said they preferred a capitalist one. Another 7 percent said that they preferred living in a communist country above all. The findings show that the percentage of millennials who prefer socialism over capitalism is a full 10 points higher than that of the general population. By comparison, over half of baby boomers polled favour capitalism, compared to 26 percent who support a socialist system.

The report also found that one in five Americans in their 20s consider former Soviet dictator Joseph Stalin a hero, despite his genocide of Ukrainians and Orthodox priests. Over a quarter of millennials polled also thought the same for Vladimir Lenin and Kim Jong Un.

One of the most troubling findings of the report is that **over 40 percent of Americans believe that there should be restrictions placed on the First Amendment and free speech to ensure that anything being said is not 'offensive.'**

The survey also uncovered that a basic working knowledge of communism among all Americans is lacking. Seven out of 10 Americans do not know the definition of communism as it is most often confused with socialism. The same amount also underestimates the number of people who have been killed by communist regimes.

'This troubling turn highlights widespread historical illiteracy in American society regarding socialism and the systemic failure of our education system to teach students about the genocide, destruction, and misery caused by communism since the Bolshevik Revolution one hundred years ago,' Smith said."[2]

Trouble ahead? What will the future look like, if we pass the baton onto a generation that's unwilling to learn from past mistakes because it wasn't within their own life experience? A generation that prefers to live by untested theories. Whenever we refuse to learn from the successes and failures of the past, it's folly. We are meant to build on the past, not be indifferent to it. Irreverence towards past achievements is like throwing the baby out with the bathwater and trying to reinvent the wheel every 30-40 years!

❖

CHAPTER 15

Sexgate & the Moral Race to the Bottom

In recent times, "Sexgate" has been a "watershed-moment," which has helped expose the sexual-deviancy of the world's elite, from Hollywood to the world of sports, big business and politics. The lynch pin for the tsunami of sexual abuse allegations was Hollywood director Harvey Weinstein (in late 2017), but it didn't stop with him and exposed many other big names worldwide.

We don't think there were any real surprise revelations, but certainly many unanswered questions. One of which was, "Why now? Why all of a sudden have Hollywood and the media grown a conscience?" Especially since Harvey Weinstein's behaviour was one of Hollywood's worst-kept-secrets and some of his abuses dated back 30 years.

Though for me, something doesn't quite ring true when the media, (which typically applauds liberal-immorality), suddenly screams, "Filth!" What's the real deal? Perhaps naughty Harvey upset some of his elite friends and in the prose of ruining his career, happily ruined many others along with his, because that dirty snowball just wouldn't stop rolling and picking up too much dirt!

The sex-card is the ultimate trump-card in today's modern lawfare (opposed to warfare). If all else fails, it's the quickest way to take down your political or business opponents. Because even if they are innocent, all the time they have a sex case against them, they'll be wrapped up in legal woes (and fees) for so long that they'll no longer pose any threat. Especially considering that *perception* is greater than reality in today's media driven world. Bad optics linger.

Yes sexual abuse is wrong, on every level. But if everyone knew decades ago, wasn't this scandal disingenuous and who stood to gain? Why didn't the media expose these open secrets a long time ago? The media fanes disgust, but who believes it? Smoke screens of defamation have always been used to divert attention to the shiny object.

The Pornification of our Culture is at Saturation Point

Yet regardless of what's really going on behind the scenes, more than anything, it put the spotlight **on the *pornification* of our culture and how it's reached saturation point. With recent studies revealing that children as young as 5-8 years, are accessing porn.** *(See our book, Sexual Madness, In a Sexually Confused World, for more statistics on this subject; published on Amazon and other retail outlets).*[1]

Take Hugh Hefner for instance, who died of natural causes recently (2017), at age 91. There were many mixed views on his legacy. Some saw it as the end of an era, and celebrated Hugh for normalizing porn by making it more mainstream and accessible. Many celebrities rushed forward with gushing tributes, but not everyone felt so adoring:

Writing her opinion piece in Glamour Magazine, Claire Heuchan wrote, **"Hugh Hefner is no 'hero' – he built an empire on misogyny... We shouldn't let the Playboy founder's death mask the fact that he normalised the sexual objectification of women."**

A **great man,** entrepreneur and innovator. Your legacy lives on.

-- Gene Simmons

Hugh Hefner was a **GIANT** in publishing, journalism, free speech & civil rights. He was a true original, and he was my friend. Rest well Hef.

-- Larry King

She went on, **"Reading all of the glowing tributes to Hugh Hefner, I wonder if some sort of collective amnesia has struck...** so many celebrations of the Playboy founder's work gloss over the sexism that was the foundation of Hefner's company. **Hugh Hefner profited from misogyny – he built an empire on it.** At the time of his death, Hefner's net worth was estimated to be £37 million...

Hefner was not, as some claim, a pioneer of the sexual revolution. There is nothing revolutionary about men

131

exploiting women... Hefner has even been embraced as an LGBT ally for featuring a transgender model in Playboy back in 1991. If Hefner was an ally, the word is meaningless. Objectifying a transwoman does not pave the road to equality for anyone.

Hugh Hefner is now being celebrated as a 'cultural icon who helped change the world' – and he did change the world, but not for the better. Hefner normalised the sexual objectification of women and paved the way to porn culture. Hefner's legacy is selling male fantasies of women's bodies and women's sexuality as 'freedom.' But really, it's just more of the same old misogyny."[2]

Fake Cultural Icon & Fake Legacy:

According to Sarah Vine from the Daily Mail, **"The way the tributes have been pouring in from assorted celebrities, you'd think he was some kind of saint...** He paved the way for the 'pornification' of day-to-day society... **Hefner's legacy is one of the most toxic in human history...** No man ever did more than Hugh Hefner to popularise the sexual exploitation of women... Quite simply, he did for sex and human relationships what Andy Warhol did to art: reduced it to the lowest common denominator, and dragged everyone else down with him."

She went on to say: "He was an icon of post-war American liberalism, the man who turned titillation into a multi-million-dollar empire, who harnessed the spirit of free love and social revolution – and slapped a pair of bunny ears on it..."

Sarah raised another valid point, which many others wouldn't have had the courage to do, concerning "the widespread notion... [made] even more dangerous by the rise of extreme Islam — that all Western women and young girls are promiscuous moral degenerates, neither deserving nor desirous of respect."

In conclusion she said, "Hefner was a very clever man. He was the first person to spot the commercial advantages of the post-war sexual revolution, to capitalise on those new-found moral freedoms and to turn women's liberation and their justifiable desire for equality against them, exploiting their sexual emancipation for his own gains.

He knew that if he dressed up age-old vice in the latest fashions — **feminism, intellectual rebellion, liberalism, a sneering disdain for conservative morality** — people would lap it up. And they did."[3]

Fake Freedom Fighter:

Contrast this with some of the adoring women whose careers went viral because of Hefner:

> RIP to the **legendary** Hugh Hefner! I'm so honoured to have been a part of the Playboy team! You will be greatly missed! Love you Hef! Xoxo.
> -- **Kim Kardashian**

> So sad to hear the news about Hugh Hefner. He was a **legend, innovator & one of a kind.** We had many fun & incredible memories together.
> -- **Paris Hilton**

He was an **American hero.** A pioneer. A kind and humble soul who opened up his life and home to the world.

-- Hefner's Widow Crystal Harris

❖

CHAPTER 16

Billy Graham
The Masterful Christian
Media Visionary

B illy Graham's favour with the press is well documented. It is said that in 1949 the attendance at Billy Graham's meetings was nominal, until certain media moguls such as: William Randolph Hearst, (head of a large publishing empire), Henry Luce, (chief of Time, Inc.), and radio personality Stuart Hamblen chose to endorse him. After which Graham's meeting attendance exploded.

According to sources, "In 1949, a group called 'Christ for Greater Los Angeles' invited Graham to preach at their L.A. revival. When radio personality Stuart Hamblen had

Graham on his radio show, word of the revival spread. **The publicity filled Graham's tents and extended the revival for an additional five weeks.** At the urging of newspaper magnate William Randolph Hearst, papers around the nation covered Graham's revival meetings closely. **As a consequence, Graham became a Christian superstar...**

The Anti-Communist Preaching Superstar:

Sociologically it is believed that Graham's success was directly related to the cultural climate of post-WWII America. **Graham spoke out against the evils of Communism** — one of the biggest fears threatening the American consciousness. In a 1954 interview Graham stated:

> Either communism must die, or Christianity must die, because it is actually a battle between Christ and anti-Christ.
>
> **-- Billy Graham**

With the advent of nuclear weapons and the demonstrated fragility of life, people turned to spirituality for comfort, and Graham illuminated their path.

Thus, Graham helped bind together a vulnerable nation through religious revival... Graham made evangelism enticing, non-threatening, even easy — and **the media made his messages accessible to the masses.**

Televangelist:

In order to expand and maintain a professional ministry, Graham and his colleagues eventually incorporated the Billy

Graham Evangelistic Association (BGEA). Graham began broadcasting his sermons over the radio... transmitted to 150 stations before reaching its peak of 1,200 stations across America.

Eventually this program was converted into a television show... The success of Graham's radio and television programs **speak to his role as a Christian media visionary. Graham used the *media* as a means for spreading the gospel of Christ, allowing him to access millions of people around the globe.**

With Graham's success, BGEA opened numerous international offices and started publishing periodicals, records, tapes, films and books... BGEA eventually began to air footage of these crusades on national television...

In 1952, the Billy Graham Evangelistic Association created the Billy Graham Evangelistic Film Ministry as a means of distributing personal conversion stories to the public through films. BGEA also acquired several radio stations around America in an effort to broadcast Graham's radio shows to a wider audience.

Print Media:

In terms of print media, BGEA created *Christianity Today* in 1955. This magazine continues to be the leading journal for evangelical Christians. In 1958, BGEA started *Decision* magazine, a monthly mailer with bible studies, articles, church histories and crusade updates. Eventually this magazine was published in Spanish, French and German.

Additionally, Graham himself authored numerous books including such titles as *Angels: God's Secret Agents* (1975), *How to be Born Again* (1979), *Death and the Life After* (1994) and *The Journey: Living by Faith in an Uncertain World* (2006)..."

Not afraid to use the media and the tools that God put at his disposal, Billy Graham skilfully got his message out and "had been rated by the Gallup organization as **'One of the Ten Most Admired Men in the World' a staggering 51 times.**"[1]

Media Mogul Instructs - "Puff Graham!"

The media has enormous power to influence and William Randolph Hearst understood this when it came to propelling Graham and his message. I believe that God alone set Billy up for success and that Graham had the ability to recognise the moment that he was in and able to skilfully catch-the-wave. He was God's man, in the right place at the right time – available and willing. God used him and the media at the same time.

Graham had his critics of course, claiming him to be too liberal and cozy with the media. I disagree. We believe that God gave Graham the wisdom and revelation to see things for what they were and use every means possible to fulfil his mission.

Confirmed by additional sources Hearst first heard Graham preach in 1949. He immediately sent word to his chain of newspapers to, **"Puff Billy Graham!"** His minions obeyed and overnight the evangelist became a household name. The news media service across America ran with the story and have followed Billy Graham ever since.

The Father of Yellow Journalism:

As the millionaire newspaper baron was such a dominating figure in 20th century communications he provided the perfect conduit for God's message. His impressive career in the media spanned newspapers, magazines, radio, broadcasting and film. It's said that he changed the face of the way mass media would be seen globally and was nicknamed, **"Father of Yellow Journalism"** for his sensationalist style of news reporting.

Sources say that he and Henry Luce, chief of Time, Inc. (another media publishing empire) made a powerful alliance when they came together to promote Graham at a time when the threat of Communism was still very fresh. Both of these influential men were deeply concerned about Communism and the growth of liberalism in the United States.

At that time Russia was testing its first atomic bomb and Graham addressed this menace in his preaching text and is quoted as saying: *"Communism is inspired and directed by the Devil himself, who has declared war against Almighty God..."*

Hearts and Luce thought they'd found a convenient propagator of their own message, in Billy Graham. Did they realise they were being used! Time was proof of how well Graham understood the role of the media in getting the message out. It required professional expertise and he was not shy of using the media for his mission from God.

❖

CHAPTER 17

Broadcasting the Truth

I AM THE GATE; whoever enters through me will be saved. They will come <u>in and go out</u>, and find pasture. The thief comes only to steal and kill and destroy; I have come that they may have life, and have it to the full (John 10:9-10 NIV emphasis added).

Your GATES shall be open continually, they shall not be shut day or night, that men may bring to you the wealth of the nations--and their kings led in procession your voluntary captives... you shall call your walls Salvation and your GATES Praise.
(Isaiah 60:11, 18 AMPC emphasis added)

Notice that Jesus is the ultimate *Gateway.* We are meant to go in and out and find pasture. We are free in Christ. John 8:36 states, "If the Son makes you free, you shall be free indeed" (NKJV).

It was for this freedom that Christ set us free [completely liberating us]; therefore keep standing firm and do not be subject again to a yoke of slavery [which you once removed].

(Galatians 5:1 AMP)

*For the law of the Spirit of life in Christ Jesus hath made me **free** from the law of sin and death.*

(Romans 8:2 KJV)

Then you will know the truth, and the truth will set you **free.**

(John 8:32 NIV)

*For the one who was a slave when called to faith in the Lord is the Lord's **freed person;** similarly, the one who was free when called is Christ's slave.*

(1 Corinthians 7:22 NIV)

Purifying the Information Flow

Why should we purify and control the information flow? Because we are meant to, "Reign in life by one, Jesus Christ" (Romans 5:17 KJV). **We are here to broadcast the good news.** Although the seven nations were stronger (Deuteronomy 7:1-2), they are not stronger than Jesus:

*Thanks be to God, who always leads us as captives in Christ's triumphal procession and **USES US TO SPREAD THE AROMA OF THE KNOWLEDGE OF HIM EVERYWHERE.***

(2 Corinthians 2:14 NIV)

In the Messiah, in Christ, God leads us from place to place in one perpetual victory parade. **Through us, he brings knowledge of Christ. Everywhere we go, people breathe in the exquisite fragrance.** *Because of Christ, we give off a sweet scent rising to God, which is recognized by those on the way of salvation — an aroma redolent with life.* **But those on the way to destruction treat us more like the stench from a rotting corpse. This is a terrific responsibility. Is anyone competent to take it on?**

(2 Corinthians 2:14-17 MSG)

Jesus wants truth broadcast across the nations, not lies, distrust and division like the devil wants, **"When he lies, he speaks his native language, for he is a liar and the father of lies"** (John 8:44 NIV).

"When the Liar speaks, he... FILLS THE WORLD WITH LIES. I arrive on the scene, tell you the plain truth, and you refuse to have a thing to do with me..." (See John 8:44-47 MSG emphasis added).

The Gateway of Truth and Revelation

Simon Peter answered and said, **Thou art the Christ, the Son of the living God.** *Jesus answered and said unto him, Blessed art thou, Simon Barjona: for flesh and blood hath not* **REVEALED** *it unto thee, but my Father which is in heaven. And I say also unto thee...* **upon this rock I will build my church; and the GATES of hell shall not prevail against it.**

(Matthew 16:16-18 KJV emphasis added)

143

The <u>shepherd</u> walks right up to the <u>gate</u>. The **GATEKEEPER** *opens the gate to him and the sheep recognize his voice. He* **calls** *his own sheep by name and* **leads** *them out. When he gets them all out,* **he leads them and they follow** *because they are familiar with his voice. They won't follow a stranger's voice but will scatter because they aren't used to the sound of it.*

I AM THE GATE for the sheep. All those others are up to no good — sheep stealers, every one of them. But the sheep didn't listen to them. I AM THE GATE...

(See John 10:1-30 MSG)

We are Destined to be Gatekeepers

Notice that Jesus is both the shepherd *and* the gate in the above scripture? Likewise, we are destined to be both sheep and to become God's gatekeepers. We start out as converts but no one stays a convert forever! As disciples we are called to be gatekeepers, who help usher in the sheep *(new converts)*. As we mature, we help shepherd God's sheep, to feed and to nurture them in the truth and revelation knowledge of Christ. Only to a disciple did Jesus instruct: "Feed my sheep" (John 21:17).

In Conclusion:

- Jesus is THE Gateway of Truth and Revelation
- We are the gatekeepers
- We are required to penetrate the culture - with God's incorruptible seed
- Media is a broadcasting platform to fill the world with truth not lies

- To enter media we need to be called and educated
- We must be divinely positioned, appointed and anointed
- Media gifts must be recognised and not churchy-fied!
- We must be humbly willing to follow and obey God's bigger strategy plan
- We are a living sacrifice

❖

CHAPTER 18

New Age in the Church

I t's true to say, in today's world, life is very hectic. Yet as believers we have a phenomenal array of technology, media and rich teachings at our disposal. There's no lack seemingly.

Preserving Spiritual Equilibrium (Balance)

Different revelations can be emphasised on, such as grace or prosperity for example and we unintentionally make superstars out of our favourite preachers and teachers. This is fine to a degree. The concern arises when we start listening to them rather than God.

In addition, when we emphasise on one revelation, *(at the exclusion of all else)*, we lose balance and become spiritually disorientated without even realizing it.

The fact is, that many churches are following New Age concepts without even knowing it and have become accustomed to using New Age philosophy and sophisticated terminology, rather than that which *lifts up* the Lord Jesus Christ.

Some churches purposely start out that way, while others evolve that way by osmosis. They slowly lose sight of the truth and blend with the culture to avoid social or emotional conflicts. Deception creeps in through lack of teaching and maturity from those who are in positions of responsibility, who forget that it's our job to, "…refute arguments and theories and reasonings and every proud and lofty thing that **sets itself up against the true knowledge of God**…" (2 Corinthians 10:5 AMPC)

> *Demolishing arguments and ideas, every high-and-mighty* **philosophy that** <u>**pits itself against the knowledge**</u> <u>**of the one true God**</u>**.** *We are taking prisoners of every thought, every emotion…*
>
> *(2 Corinthians 10:5 VOICE)*

> *The tools of our trade aren't for… manipulation, but they are for* **demolishing that entire massively corrupt culture.** *We use our powerful God-tools for smashing* **warped philosophies, tearing down barriers** <u>**erected**</u> <u>**against the truth of God**</u>**,** *fitting every loose thought* **and emotion and impulse** *into the structure of life shaped by Christ. Our tools are ready at hand for clearing the ground of every obstruction and building lives of* **obedience into maturity.**
>
> *(2 Corinthians 10:3-6 MSG)*

The Doctrine of Demons

The infiltration of the doctrine of demons is nothing new to the church: "The wisdom of this world should never be mistaken for heavenly wisdom; **it originates below in the earthly realms, with the demons,**" (James 3:15 VOICE); "This superficial wisdom is not such as comes down from above, but is earthly, unspiritual (animal), even devilish (demoniacal)" (James 3:15 AMPC); "This wisdom descendeth not from above, but is earthly, sensual, devilish" (KJVS).

Notice that this counterfeit and devilish knowledge/ wisdom wants one thing only; "**...to set itself up against the knowledge of God.**" And if it goes unchallenged, will indeed succeed in establishing itself as the acceptable *truth* of the culture. **Embedded into society via the educational systems and social media for example.**

My wife Jennifer has recently written a book about this subject and one particular chapter she entitled, "Tolerance the god of this Age sits on the Throne of Culture" *(I recommend that you read it! Millennial Myopia, from a Biblical Perspective; published on Amazon and other retail outlets).*[1]

However, I would suggest, that **losing sight of the cross** is one of the biggest dangers that we face, especially as believers. Scripture clearly teaches that we must, "take up our crosses daily." Something that is done "daily" determines "lifestyle." Therefore taking up our crosses daily, points to a surrendered lifestyle.

Anyone who intends to come with me has to let me lead. You're not in the driver's seat---I am. Don't *run from suffering; embrace it. Follow me and I'll show you how. <u>Self-help is no help at all.</u>*

Self-sacrifice is the way, my way, to finding yourself, your true self. What good would it do to get everything you want and lose you, the real you? If any of you is embarrassed with me and the way I'm leading you, know that the Son of Man will be far more embarrassed with you when he arrives in all his splendor in company with the Father and the holy angels.

(Luke 9:23-27 MSG)

See just how counter cultural this is? **"Self help is no help at all."** Try telling that to this narcissistic generation, who are totally surrendered to their emotions and feelings and any thought of "self denial" would be considered "abusive!" As believers, we are not swayed by the culture, we have God's Word to go on, not our feelings. So let's just take a look to see where we may need to adjust our thinking and experience Christ anew with fresh revelation.

What does The New Age really look Like?

It's rather hard to define or neatly package into one simple definition. In fact it's very *nebulous*, meaning that it's so vast in its own concepts that it's purposely vague and ambiguous. It would take copious amounts of ink and paper to try and we're not willing to devote that much time to it!

The basic premise is that man wants to achieve his own state of goodness, one that he can control and determine. Just like running after the *things* of God without running after God Himself. Having a form of religion but denying the power of it. Even attempting to become greater than Christ Himself.

❖

CHAPTER 19

Self-Deification

This leads me to *apotheosis* or *self-deification*. One psychologist recently wrote:

Self-deification is the perfect antidote for feeling inadequate. It's much simpler than learning or growing. Don't improve; prove! Prove you're a god!

-- Jeremy E Sherman Ph.D.

Recently we had a paper submitted to our University, by one of our students (Rev Benjamin Noumba Mbock – Cameroon) in Africa, about the growth of the church, and the influence of the New Age in the African church. It's one of the best papers we've ever read from one of our students, from an African perspective. Which is important to us, as we're called to work with the African church all over the world.

His paper concerned the genuine growth of the African church versus the influence of the New Age movement. Now not many associate the African church with the New Age movement, but as a mature minister, this particular student laid out his argument very well; it was a compelling read.

One would associate witchcraft with Africa but not necessarily the New Age, which is more of a Western enterprise *(albeit the same thing - witchcraft)*, it's just branded differently. It's a bit more sophisticated and palatable for European gentry perhaps, than the local African village witch doctor!

He talked about the growth numbers in the African church not being authentic and that the New Age has infiltrated the African church, with many pastors teaching New Age philosophy rather than scripture and revelation.

Philosophies are more acceptable than the Truth!

Those responsible in our churches worldwide have a responsibility to teach God's Word, first and foremost. Whether it's from an African viewpoint or any other, the fact is that the whole world is being impacted by deception and **many pastors are teaching New Age, self-help concepts, psychology and philosophy, because it's more** *acceptable* **to the general public.**

> One of the biggest advantages we have as New Agers is once the occult, metaphysical, and New Age terminology is removed **we have concepts and techniques that are very** <u>acceptable</u> **to the general public**.
>
> -- **Dick Sutphen**

Jesus and His message were always counter-cultural, from a secular point of view, but even now within the growing church culture and the media.

When we are preferring the culture, to the Spirit of God, that's when we side with it. We can reach the culture without siding with it. Of course God wants to reach into secular culture and reach every generation but we must side with God and His truth every time, **"His truth endureth to *all* generations"** (Psalm 100:5 KJVS). "Suppose ye that I am come to give peace on earth? I tell you, Nay; but rather division" (Luke 12:51 KJV).

Is Racism in the Church?

Yes! We are called to the African church. Every country we arrive in, we end up preaching to Africans. But it saddens us to see that others are not willing to cross-pollinate the same way. They remain colour-bound. We choose to remain colour-blind and go where God tells us, because His kingdom thrives on diversity. We should have Chinese, Spanish, Italian, American, African, British, German and Belgians etc., in our churches. That's kingdom!

Leaders who are not called by God

There are many pastors leading churches today, who are not even called by God to be in that position. They are too easily threatened and can't relate to other leaders outside of their ego-bubble. They start churches in pursuit of self-aggrandisement.

In Italy we have 100s of isolated little churches and we see pastors continuing to struggle. In many cases they are supposedly *relating* to some bishop or apostle in Africa somewhere, but really they're just being *pimped* for money. It's fake piety and a religious brand of trafficking.

That's extreme! Yes it is. It's prostituting the church for profit: **"Perverse** disputings of men of corrupt minds, and destitute of the truth, **supposing that gain is godliness:** from such withdraw thyself. But godliness with contentment is great gain" (1 Timothy 6:5-6 KJV).

We've seen men raised up into positions of leadership that they were never appointed by God to be in. They belong in the market place (and vice versa). They bring out books and perform power-point messages in churches all over the world, but there's no *power* to any of it. They dress right, sound right, look right - but it's all wrong!

Lust is Rampant

We've gone to churches where *lust* is rife. Evidenced in the way that people dress. Look around; see the flirtatious and tight fitting clothes on both men and women, either too tight or cut too low. It's a secular social club mentality with a bit of church culture mixed in. We've preached in churches where it was revealed to me that homosexuals were leading the choir and female prostitutes were regular members of the choir! This too was common knowledge to the elders, who met regularly for *tricks* after church. Why is this happening? It's because there's no emphasis on holiness in these places. *We are talking about church people!*

Recently in a viral and passionate Facebook Live video, Juanita Bynum called out all "scantily dressed female

156

ministers," and told them to put some clothes on saying: *"How are you coming to church on a Sunday morning to worship God and you have no bra on?"* She had so much more to say, but she certainly has a point.[1]

The right spirit always applauds Truth

Many won't like what we're saying here, but those with a true spirit will always applaud the truth. Always remember God's yoke is easy, He is great, but the devil is always a liar. They are *not* equal opposites. There is no yin and yang. God is mighty.

❖

CHAPTER 20

What it Means
To be Born-Again

In this last chapter let's remind ourselves what it means to be born-again. We ask Jesus Christ to come into our lives as our Lord and Saviour – (John 3:3,5-8,15-21 KJVS).

"Jesus answered and said unto him, Verily, verily, I say unto thee, Except a man be *born again,* he cannot see the kingdom of God… Verily, verily, I say unto thee, Except a man be born of water and of the Spirit, he cannot enter into the kingdom of God. That which is born of the flesh is flesh; and that which is *born of the Spirit* is spirit. *Marvel not that I said unto thee, Ye must be born again.* The wind bloweth where it listeth, and thou hearest the sound thereof, but canst not tell whence it cometh, and whither it goeth: so is every one that is *born of the Spirit...*"

That whosoever believeth in him should not perish, but have eternal life. For God so loved the world, that he gave his only begotten Son, that whosoever believeth in him should not perish, but have everlasting life. **For God sent not his Son into the world to condemn the world; but that the world through him might be saved.**

He that believeth on him is not condemned: but he that believeth not is condemned already, because he hath not believed in the name of the only begotten Son of God. And this is the condemnation, that light is come into the world, and men loved darkness rather than light, because their deeds were evil. For every one that doeth evil hateth the light, neither cometh to the light, lest his deeds should be reproved. **But he that doeth truth cometh to the light, that his deeds may be made manifest, that they are wrought in God.**

The True Sons of God and our Free Will

However the same bible that tell us, "For by grace are ye saved through faith; and that not of yourselves: it is the gift of God: Not of works, lest any man should boast" (Ephesians 2:8-9 KJVS); also tells us, "Work out your own salvation with fear and trembling" (Philippians 2:12 KJVS).

This is because grace doesn't negate personal responsibility, "He that hath my commandments, **and keepeth them,** he it is that loveth me: and he that loveth me shall be loved of my Father, and I will love him, and will manifest myself to him" (John 14:21 KJVS).

Yes salvation is by grace through faith, but this doesn't make repentance redundant either. Jesus preached repentance and the kingdom of God. True Christianity is a life of obedience, in the pursuit of true maturity, without an orphan spirit:

> *For as many as are led by the Spirit of God, they are the sons of God. For ye have not received the spirit of bondage again to fear; but ye have received the Spirit of adoption, whereby we cry, Abba, Father. The Spirit itself beareth witness with our spirit, that we are the children of God:*
>
> *(Romans 8:14-16 KJVS)*

Sanctification is a process, therefore there's none of us who aren't still a *work in progress*. And since sin is conceived in our souls and not in our spirits, the soul acts like a pendulum, swinging between the spirit and the flesh. Why? Because having a free-will means the choice is always ours, "I have set before you life and death, blessing and cursing: **therefore choose life…**" (Deuteronomy 30:19 KJVS)

"Father, if thou be willing, remove this cup from me: nevertheless **not my will, but thine, be done**" (Luke 22:42 KJVS). In this very instance Jesus demonstrated a *surrendered* free will.

So our flesh is not born again, it's perishing and getting older. We don't get a new body until we receive our resurrection bodies: (Philippians 3:21; 1 Corinthians 15:35; Revelation 21:4; 1 Corinthians 15:43, 44, 53).

It is the same with the resurrection of the dead. What is
sown is perishable, what is raised is imperishable.
(1 Corinthians 15:42 NET)

Christ died on the cross so that we could be forgiven
and the temple veil was torn in two, symbolising access
was granted to the Holy of Holies. Jesus is our eternal Way
Maker. "I am the way, the truth, and the life: no man cometh
unto the Father, but by me" (John 14:6 KJVS).

Our soul and flesh benefit from God's indwelling
presence in our lives. We are earthen vessels, who have been
broken before Him, so that He can minister to us and through
us.

Why broken? Let me make it very clear, the flesh
is wicked: "The heart is deceitful above all things, and
desperately wicked: who can know it?" (Jeremiah 17:9 KJVS)

True Understanding versus Vain Imaginations

When they knew God, they glorified him not as God, neither
*were thankful; but **became vain in their imaginations**,*
and their foolish heart was darkened.
(Romans 1:21 KJVS)

I have always enjoyed the way that Smith Wigglesworth
described faith. And I have quoted him below. But let us
not be accused, in this generation, of wanting the *things* of
Christ without wanting Christ in person; of worshipping
our own imaginations and striving to *get* and *accumulate*
things rather than taking up our crosses daily and letting
Him take the wheel.

If we *must* be ambitious for anything, let it be for truth and understanding. Especially understanding: **"With all thy getting get understanding,"** (Proverbs 4:7 KJVS); "Buy the truth, and sell it not; also wisdom, and instruction, and understanding" (Proverbs 23:23 KJVS).

The context for this is that we must have a foundation of knowledge for everything that we say. As preachers, we must never just preach what we *think*. Anyone can *think!* We must go beyond mere *thinking*. Instead we must say what we *know*. And base nothing on wild assumptions, vain imaginations, not even educated guesses.

> Let go of your own thoughts, and take the thoughts of God, the Word of God. **If you build yourself on imaginations you will go wrong.** You have the Word of God and it's enough.
>
> **-- Smith Wigglesworth**

Knowing God by His Word

All lack of faith is due to not feeding on God's Word. You need it every day. Feed on the living Christ of whom this Word is full. As you get taken up with the glorious fact that the wondrous presence of the living Christ, **the faith of God will spring up within you.**

If I am going to know God, I am going to know him by His Word. I know I shall be in heaven, but I could not build on my feeling that I am going to heaven. I am going to heaven because God's Word

says it and I believe God's Word. **"Faith comes by hearing and hearing by the Word of God."**
-- Smith Wigglesworth

❖

Endnotes

Chapter 1 Spiritual Gateway

1. Strong's Hebrew Concordance with KJV. Taken from the TecartaBible App, © 2017 Tecarta, Inc. Version 7.11.5. Used by permission. All rights reserved.

2. Brown-Driver-Briggs' Hebrew and English Lexicon, ISBN-13: 978-1565632066, Publisher: Hendrickson Pub; Reprint edition (June 1, 1996).

Chapter 2 The Definition of Media

1. https://www.investopedia.com/articles/investing/061115/googles-revenue-beats-gdp-several-major-countries.asp?ad=dirN&qo=investopediaSiteSearch&qsrc=0&o=40186

2. https://en.oxforddictionaries.com/definition/groupthink

Chapter 4 Cultivate Divine Connections

1. http://www.foxnews.com/shows/ingraham-angle.html

2. http://www1.cbn.com/cbnnews/us/2017/october/how-trump-remade-the-reagan-revolution-in-his-own-image

Chapter 5 As Goes America, So Goes the World

1. http://www.washingtontimes.com/news/2017/may/23/how-much-does-cnn-hate-trump-93-of-coverage-is-neg/

2. http://www.chicagotribune.com/news/columnists/kass/ct-trump-media-coverage-harvard-kass-0521-20170519-column.html

3. KYLE SMITH September 20, 2017, http://www.nationalreview.com/article/451550/hillary-new-lies-lies-lies-list-grows-longer

4. ANDREW C. MCCARTHY October 29, 2016, http://www.nationalreview.com/article/441573/hillary-clinton-corruption-foundation

Chapter 6 Collusion and the Jezebel Spirit

1. https://study.com/academy/lesson/adversarial-journalism-definition-history.html

2. http://www.nationalreview.com/article/450906/antifa-berkeley-protest-turns-violent-again

3. For more see UrbanDictionary.com, https://www.urbandictionary.com/define.php?term=Antifa

Chapter 7 Promoting Diversity or Global Homogenization?

1. https://www.naturalnews.com/022967_milk_pasteurization_dairy.html

Chapter 8 Democracy Debunked

1. https://townhall.com/tipsheet/christinerousselle/2017/10/30/dnc-email-straight-white-men-need-not-apply-n2402482, Christine Rousselle, Posted Oct 30, 2017

Chapter 9 The Media & Artificial Intelligence in the End Times Part 1

1. https://en.oxforddictionaries.com/definition/artificial_intelligence

2. By Lauren Tousignant, New York Post, http://www.foxnews.com/tech/2017/10/27/this-artificial-intelligence-may-start-tracking-soon.html

3. https://en.wikipedia.org/wiki/Orwellian

4. http://www.telegraph.co.uk/news/uknews/6210255/EU-funding-Orwellian-artificial-intelligence-plan-to-monitor-public-for-abnormal-behaviour.html

5. https://www.theguardian.com/technology/2017/mar/13/artificial-intelligence-ai-abuses-fascism-donald-trump

Chapter 10 The Media & Artificial Intelligence in the End Times Part 2

1. https://www.taylorwessing.com/download/article-robo journalism-ai-and-the-media.html

2. Kamal Ahmed Business editor September 2015, http://www.bbc.com/news/business-34266425

3. https://www.inverse.com/article/34629-mark-cuban-artificial-intelligence-jobs

4. https://www.cnbc.com/2017/07/25/mark-cuban-on-ai-it-scares-me.html

5. https://www.cnbc.com/2017/07/25/mark-cuban-on-ai-it-scares-me.html

Chapter 11 The Global Phenomena of Facebook & Social Media

1. By Timothy B. Leetim@vox.com, June 28, 2017, https://www.vox.com/new-money/2017/6/28/15873876/mark-zuckerberg-for-president

2. By Ethan Huff, Thursday, August 10, 2017, https://www.naturalnews.com/2017-08-10-diamond-and-silk-youtube-google-facebook-on-black-censorship-rampage-to-silence-all-pro-trump-voices.html

3. https://www.washingtontimes.com/news/2017/aug/10/diamond-and-silk-rip-youtube-say-95-of-videos-demo/

4. http://www1.cbn.com/cbnnews/world/2017/october/christians-are-being-told-to-shut-up-expelled-student-who-called-homosexuality-a-sin-loses-court-case

5. By Chris Ciaccia, Fox News, http://www.foxnews.com/tech/2017/11/09/former-facebook-exec-sean-parker-says-god-only-knows-what-its-doing-to-our-childrens-brains.html

6. https://www.axios.com/sean-parker-unloads-on-facebook-2508036343.html

Chapter 12 What the Psychologists are Saying about Facebook

1. Douglas T. Kenrick Ph.D., Post on psychologytoday coauthored by Jessica E. Bodford, Posted April 11, 2014, https://www.psychologytoday.com/blog/sex-murder-and-the-meaning-life/201404/7-ways-facebook-is-bad-your-mental-health

2. Alice G. Walton - contributor, https://www.forbes.com/sites/alicegwalton/2017/06/30/a-run-down-of-social-medias-effects-on-our-mental-health/#fb25f22e5afa

3. http://www.bbc.com/news/technology-23709009

4. Damien Pearse Sat 17 March 2012 13.41 GMT, https://www.theguardian.com/technology/2012/mar/17/facebook-dark-side-study-aggressive-narcissism

Chapter 13 Google The Largest Country in the World

1. By Scott Cleland and Contributor Ira Brodsky, https://www.goodreads.com/book/show/11229002-search-destroy

2. 9:08 AM ET Tue, 27 June 2017, 00:45, https://www.cnbc.com/2017/06/27/eu-hits-google-with-a-record-antitrust-fine-of-2-point-7-billion.html, Karen Gilchrist, Anita Balakrishnan

Chapter 14 Socialism Creating the Ultimate Safe-Space

1. https://www.merriam-webster.com/dictionary/socialism

2. http://www.foxnews.com/us/2017/11/03/millennials-think-socialism-would-create-great-safe-space-study-finds.html

Chapter 15 Sexgate & the Moral Race to the Bottom

1. Sexual Madness, In a Sexually Confused World, by Doctors Alan and Jennifer Pateman, ISBN: 978-1-909132-02-3, available from Amazon and other retail outlets: https://www.amazon.co.uk/Alan-Pateman/e/B00JHVDBPO

2. By Claire Heuchan, 28 September 2017, http://www.glamourmagazine.co.uk/article/hugh-hefner-sexist

3. By Sarah Vine September 2017, http://www.dailymail.co.uk/news/article-4931620/Hero-No-Hugh-Hefner-s-legacy-utterly-toxic-women.html#ixzz4yD4MghFs

Endnotes

Chapter 16 Billy Graham The Masterful Christian Media Visionary

1. Billy Graham, Biography.com, https://www.biography.com/people/billy-graham-9317669 2017

Chapter 18 New Age in the Church

1. Millennial Myopia, From a Biblical Perspective, by Doctor Jennifer Pateman, ISBN: 978-1-909132-67-2, available from Amazon and other retail outlets: https://www.amazon.co.uk/Jennifer-Pateman/e/B077VV4M2G

Chapter 19 Self-Deification

1. https://www.youtube.com/watch?v=oa2UPbcXbBc

Bible translations

- Scripture references marked AMP are taken from The Amplified Bible. Old Testament copyright © 1965, 1987 by Zondervan Corporation, Grand Rapids, Michigan. New Testament copyright © 1958, 1987 by The Lockman Foundation, La Habra, California. All rights reserved.

- Scripture references marked AMPC are taken from the Amplified® Bible (AMPC), Copyright © 1954, 1958, 1962, 1964, 1965, 1987 by The Lockman Foundation. Used by permission. www.Lockman.org

- Scripture references marked KJV are taken from the King James Version of the bible.

- Scripture references marked KJVS are taken from the Strong's Concordance with KJV. Taken from the TecartaBible App, © 2017 Tecarta, Inc. Version 7.11.5. Used by permission. All rights reserved.

- Scripture references marked MSG are taken from The Message. Copyright © 1993, 1994, 1995, 1996, 2000, 2001, 2002. Used by permission of NavPress Publishing Group.

- Scripture references marked NET are taken from the NET Bible® Copyright ©1996-2006 by Biblical Studies Press, L.L.C. http://netbible.com All rights reserved.

❖

Ministry Profile - Dr Alan

Doctor Alan Pateman, an apostle, is the President and Founder of **"Alan Pateman Ministries International"** (APMI), which was established in England back in 1987, a Christian-based *(parachurch)* non-profit and non-denominational outreach. This ministry is now focusing in two main areas: First **"Connecting for Excellence"** Apostolic Networking (CFE) and secondly, the teaching arm, **"LifeStyle International Christian University"** (LICU).

CFE is a multi-facetted missions organisation with the purpose of connecting leaders for divine opportunities and building lasting relationships, to touch the lives of leaders literally the world over. Apostle Dr Alan Pateman has to date ordained more than 500 ministers in over 50 NATIONS. In addition there are ministries, churches and schools who are in Association or Affiliation, looking to him for apostolic counsel and oversight.

Secondly LICU, which was founded in 2007, is a study program to help people discover their purpose and destiny. A global network of university campuses and correspondence students, demonstrating the Supernatural Kingdom of God through Doctrinal, Apostolic and Prophetic Teaching. Dr Alan holds the position of President/CEO, Professor of Theology, Biblical Studies and Apostolic Ministry. LICU is exploding throughout Europe, Asia and Africa, enhancing the Body of Christ

Dr Alan has authored more than 40 books including numerous teaching materials and LICU university courses (30) along with hundreds of Truth for the Journey articles on kingdom lifestyle *(that are regularly distributed globally via the internet).*

He is recognised as an Apostle, Bishop, Leadership Mentor, University Educator, Motivational Speaker, Connector and Author, who has also been featured on national and international TV and radio networks throughout the years.

Currently Apostle Alan, his wife Dr Jennifer reside in Lucca *(Tuscany)* Italy and travel out from their Apostolic Company.

- Alan Pateman Ph.D., D.Min., D.D., M.A., B.Th.

Academic Background

Dr. Alan Pateman attended several colleges throughout his training *(including studying Theology at Roffey Place, Horsham, UK and a Member of Kerygma - with Rev. Colin Urquhart and Dr. Bob Gordon - 1985-1987)* before being awarded a Doctorate of Divinity *(2006)* in recognition of his lifetime achievements by the International College of Excellence, now "DanEl Christian College" *(President: Dr. Robb Thompson USA)* also "Life Christian University" *(Dr. Douglas Wingate USA)* where he also earned a Bachelor of Theology B.Th. *(2006)*, a Master of Arts in Theology M.A., a Doctor of Ministry in Theology D.Min., *(2007)* and Doctor of Philosophy in Theology Ph.D. *(2013)* from LICU.

❖

Ministry Profile - Dr Jennifer

Apostle Doctor Jennifer Pateman's passion is to see the Body of Christ equipped and walking in spiritually maturity, through a married dependency on God's Spirit and Word. Her teaching ministry has a distinct prophetic flavour and she desires to see people of all ages succeed in their God given lanes.

Officially Jennifer is the Vice President of **Alan Pateman Ministries** (APMI) and Co-Founder of **Connecting for Excellence** (CFE) and **LifeStyle International Christian University** (LICU). She is a five-fold teaching gift to the Body of Christ, author, musician, public speaker, lecturer and researcher. Apart from travelling internationally alongside her husband, she is also on the Board of Executives and functions as the Executive Dean of LICU; also holding the position of Professor of Theology, Biblical Studies, and Pastoral Ministry.

Most importantly Dr Jennifer is devoted to her Man of God and three beautiful children; they reside in Lucca, Italy and travel out from their Apostolic Company.

- Jennifer Pateman Ph.D., D.Min., D.D., M.A., B.Th.

Academic Background

Dr. Jennifer Pateman has gained her Bachelor of Christian Theology B.Th., Master of Arts in Christian Theology M.A., Doctor of Divinity D.D., Doctor of Ministry D.Min., Doctor of Philosophy in Theology Ph.D. via the following institutes: International College of Excellence *(USA, Principal Dr. Robb Thompson)*, Life Christian University *(USA, Principal Dr. Douglas Wingate)*, LifeStyle International Christian University.

❖

To Contact the Authors

Please email:

Alan Pateman Ministries International

Email: apostledr@alanpateman.com
Email: drjennifer@alanpatemanministries.com
Web: www.AlanPatemanMinistries.com

*Please include your prayer requests
and comments when you write.*

❖

Other Books

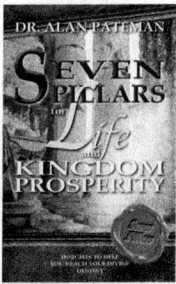

Seven Pillars for Life and Kingdom Prosperity

I submit these "Seven Pillars for Life and Kingdom Prosperity" to you, (Love, Prayer, Righteousness, Obedience, Connections, Management, Money). It's my desire that you walk in the triumphs that God has ordained for you.

ISBN: 978-1-909132-46-7, Pages: 220,
Format: Paperback, Published: 2016
Also available in eBook format!

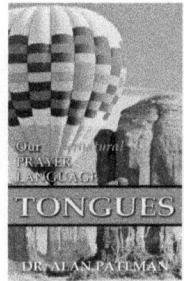

TONGUES, Our Supernatural Prayer Language

In writing to the church at Corinth, Paul encouraged them to continue the practice of speaking with other tongues in their worship of God and in their prayer lives as a means of spiritual edification. "He that speaketh in an unknown tongue edifies, charges, builds himself up like a battery."

ISBN: 978-1-909132-44-3, Pages: 144,
Format: Paperback, Published: 2016
Also available in eBook format!

Truth for the Journey Books

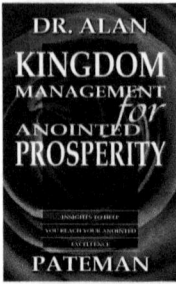

Kingdom Management for Anointed Prosperity

In his book, "Kingdom Management for Anointed Prosperity," Dr. Alan Pateman reveals how we can avoid living in continual crisis due to mismanagement. Life happens to all of us, but how we handle it matters most. "Well done, good and faithful servant! You have been faithful with a few things; I will put you in charge [as manager] of many things. Come and share your master's happiness!" (Matthew 25:21)

ISBN: 978-1-909132-34-4, Pages: 144,
Format: Paperback, Published: 2015
Also available in eBook format!

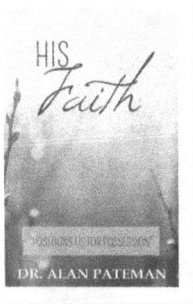

Seduction & Control:
Infiltrating Society & the Church

This book is a glance into the world of seduction and control, how they try to influence the Church through many powerful avenues such as the New Age, sexual education in our schools, basic entertainment; things that touch our everyday lives in order that we effectively and gradually become desensitised.

ISBN: 978-1-909132-00-9, Pages: 156
Format: Paperback, Published: 2015
Also available in eBook format!

His Faith Positions us for Possession

It is with both simplicity and seasoned proficiency that Dr. Pateman draws us into this weighty conclusion; ...only as we yield and surrender to Christ's faith IN us – will we truly be empowered to live as Christ lived on this earth, "...as he is, so are we in this world" *(1 John 4:17)*.

ISBN: 978-0-9570654-0-6, Pages: 128,
Format: Paperback, Published: 2014
Also available in eBook format!

WINNING by Mastering your Mind

Someone once said, "Happiness begins between your ears and your mind is the drawing room for tomorrow's circumstances..." Remember, what happens in your mind will happen in time, and therefore one of our first priorities must be mind-management.

ISBN: 978-1-909132-40-5, Pages: 136, Format: Paperback, Published: 2017
Also available in eBook format!

Sexual Madness: In a Sexually Confused World

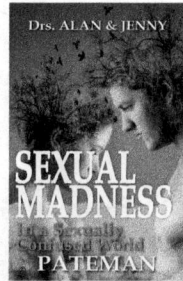

This book discusses the sensitive subject of political correctness in our world today and the growing fear of causing offence in the public arena. It also discusses the rise of homosexuality, pedophilia and all other forms of sexuality, as there are many. Including modern statistics on pornography.

ISBN: 978-1-909132-02-3, Pages: 160, Format: Paperback, Published: 2012
Also available in eBook format!

Millennial Myopia, From a Biblical Perspective

The standard for every generation is Jesus. However Millennial Myopia describes the trap of focusing everything on one particular generation or demographic cohort, at the exclusion and expense of all others. The Church cannot afford to make this mistake too. Loaded with research, this book takes readers on a journey of discovery, revealing the true nature of kingdom diversity.

ISBN: 978-1-909132-67-2, Pages: 216, Format: Paperback, Published: 2017
Also available in eBook format!

Dear Friends,

Have you considered becoming one of our international students? We are privileged to welcome you, from around the world, to "LifeStyle International Christian University" *(the teaching arm of Alan Pateman Ministries International)*. **An English speaking university** dedicated to your success; to see you trained and equipped to fully succeed in your God given Destiny.

It is our passion to raise up the leaders of tomorrow, who will have influence in all realms of authority, including the Body of Christ. Men and women of strategy, wisdom and true godliness, who'll stand with stature and maturity in this hour.

It's undeniable that in today's world, recognised education has become indispensable, therefore it is our desire to offer well balanced and well structured courses. Those that have been written by gifted and talented ministers of God, who seek to be inspired by God's Holy Spirit.

Consequently we have put together a **flexible curriculum,** designed both for correspondence students and campuses, which is a strategy to reach the distant learner; whether provincial, national or international. In fact we have many correspondence students from around the world, including a growing number of successful campuses, in various countries.

This is a growing platform, where men and women of dignity and passion, can grow and be established in their God given endeavours. As God is the healer of the nations, we pray and believe that many of our alumni will go on to **become world changers** in their own right.

We are proud of each and every one of our LICU students.
It would be our pleasure if you would join them on this incredible journey!

Doctor Alan Pateman

For more information visit our website/facebook or contact our office, using the details below:

Website: www.licuuniversity.com
Facebook: www.facebook.com/LICUMainCampus
Email: info@licuuniversity.com
Telephone: +39 366 329 1315

Alan Pateman Ministries
Presents

Conference

CONNECTING FOR
EXCELLENCE Lucca Italy

An international apostolic
and prophetic network

YOUR HOSTS: ALAN PATEMAN   JENNIFER PATEMAN

Please contact our office or download the registration form.
Registration fee: €40

apostledr@alanpateman.com, Tel. 0039 366 329 1315

WWW.ALANPATEMANMINISTRIES.COM

All Books Available

at

APMI PUBLICATIONS

Email: publications@alanpateman.com
*Also Available from Amazon.com
and other retail outlets.*

*If you purchased this book through Amazon.com
or other and enjoyed reading it, or perhaps one of
my other books, I would be grateful if you could
take a couple of minutes to write a Customer
Review, many thanks.*

www.ingramcontent.com/pod-product-compliance
Lightning Source LLC
Chambersburg PA
CBHW050119280326
41933CB00010B/1169